'ALLO 'A...

THE COMPLETE WAR DIARIES OF RENÉ ARTOIS

Based on the
BBC Television series
by Jeremy Lloyd and
David Croft

Edited and with introductions by
René Fairfax

Translated by John Haselden

Torcroft Lodges

Baln

Inv

BBC Books

Published by BBC Books,
a division of BBC Enterprises Limited,
Woodlands, 80 Wood Lane, London W12 0TT

Volume One first published in hardback 1988
Volume Two first published in hardback 1989
This combined edition first published in paperback 1991

ISBN 0 563 36327 4
Cover and page design concept: Hammond Hammond
French artwork in Volume One: John Davies
Illustrations Volume Two: Jean Hurd, Tuola Antonakes,
Larry Rostant, Oonah O'toole, Robert Gage

Set in 11/13pt Century Bold

Printed and Bound in Great Britain by
Butler & Tanner Ltd, Frome
Cover printed in England by Clays Ltd, St Ives plc

INTRODUCTION

I never met René Artois, although even before the discovery of these priceless papers I felt I had known him almost as a father.

My mother Yvette spoke about him often, of course. They fought side by side in those terrible years during the war, to free themselves from the yoke of the oppressor. And even when René's wife was not there, there were the Germans to worry about.

We share the same name. But there is more to it than that. We share the same spirit. As I left my job at the Bank of Westphalia each evening to study these diaries and arrange them for publication, I would feel the stirrings of adventure. Even so, I went straight back to my rooms and read more of René's entries, and was sometimes up late into the night.

Though these pages are shot through with his characteristic modesty, there emerges, as my mother said, something remarkable, something incredible.

Consider his position. My mother often did. At the beginning of the war, he was, like many young Frenchmen, in his mid-forties. Vital, attractive, blessed with unbounded energy and courage, he dreamed of

military service. Fortunately, someone was always there to wake him with a large cognac and remind him that he was already serving France in the best way he could. There were so many who depended upon him.

There was his wife, Edith, for a start. Although it is typical of René's generosity that she rarely came first. There was her mother, Fanny, lying desperately sick in a bed upstairs. He was constantly trying to think of ways to ease her passing. There were Carstairs and Fairfax*, the British airmen, who would be lucky to get out of the Café René alive. And there was Maria, my mother Yvette, and so many others. No matter what he had on, he would always do his best to look after them personally. He was that sort of man.

Seen in this light, it is even more extraordinary that he managed at once to keep his end up with the Resistance, to handle the Germans and to keep in good spirits all those who came to drink at his café.

René Artois passed away in 1985, and my mother, who was with him, told me with a wistful smile that he died as he had lived. He amassed a considerable fortune in later years. Not only did the hotel trade reward him handsomely, but after the war he also developed widespread and varied business interests. His dealings in the world of fine art and cuckoo clocks alone took him as far afield as Switzerland and South America.

It surprised me to learn, therefore, that his sole bequest to my mother was a rather mature knockwurst sausage, which had hung in his cellar since late 1945. My mother, however, could not have been more pleased. With a twinkle in her eye she said simply: 'He wanted me to have a little something to remember him by.' Little? That

---

* *Fairfax finally escaped to England in 1973. René had been telling him for years that the war was over, but for some reason he carried on hiding in and around the café through the fifties and sixties. He was there so long that my mother eventually married him out of sympathy and, as a result, I bear the unfortunate man's surname. I keep meaning to have it changed.*

sausage must have been a metre long. And then I
understood. René Artois could have left Yvette jewellery;
he could have left her money; but he chose instead to leave
her a piece of history. Not for him the easy gesture.

How much history I was only to find out some years
later. By time his exploits had become legendary in
France, and also in some areas of England, through
television. It was in April of last year, I remember, that I
stayed late one night at the office, working with one of the

*René Artois in
the process of
changing
history*

secretaries. She was a young girl and had much to learn, so I did not arrive home until after midnight. For some reason I still had an incredible appetite, so I went immediately to the kitchen of my mother. Alas, she had been entertaining, so René's sausage was the only thing in the larder.

I looked upon it as I often had, with respect, mixed with a certain awe. It really was a magnificent sausage, despite its age. I thought again, he must have been a remarkable man. But I was hungry and, as René himself would have said: 'When a Frenchman hungers, he must satisfy himself.' So I took that sausage, and cut myself a large slice. I must say that first mouthful tasted good. As I chewed it over, however, I detected a certain fibrous texture which, though not unpleasant, meant that my dinner lasted rather longer than I had planned. On closer inspection of the remainder of the sausage, I suddenly saw why.

Mon Dieu!

I called my mother.

It was an emotional scene. When she came upon René's sausage, now, sadly, shorter by some ten centimetres, it brought tears to her eyes.

'Mother,' I said, 'what is it?'

She, too, looked more closely, and saw that the knockwurst was not what it seemed. Concealed beneath its greying skin was a work of art of inestimable value.

'René!' she cried. 'You have just taken a very large nibble out of the Fallen Madonna with the Big Boobies by Van Clomp!'

But no.

I had consumed several thousand words of the first volume of *The War Diaries of René Artois*, which sharp-sighted readers will realise explains certain unfortunate gaps in the text that follows.

The rest, of course, is history.

René Fairfax
September 1988

1 JANUARY

What an evening! Awoke with a very stiff

my dear Edith

sharp tap with a metal spoon

dropped off.

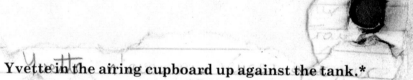

Yvette in the airing cupboard up against the tank.*

---

* *This page is considerably damaged. It is clear from the evidence that
remains, however, that René began the year as he meant to go on. He
was a man of great stamina. Aroused after the night's traditional
festivities, he discovers a large cognac on his bedside table. Why it
is stiff can only be guessed at, though my mother recalls that he
promised to give her one the previous day and wanted it close to hand.*

  *In any event, we move on with a word or two of culinary advice
from Le Grand Chef to his lady wife, before he decides to have a little
lie-in.*

  *The entry concludes with René and Yvette making a bold attack
on a Panzer. From the upstairs bathroom of the café it would have
been possible for René to lob a grenade through the skylight and down
into the street. He must have asked my mother to help prime his
weapon in the airing cupboard prior to launching a vigorous assault.*

2 JANUARY

and most of the day sleeping it off. I hope, dear diary, that this is not a sign of things to come.

But what sort of year will it be, I wonder, under the tyranny of the jackboot? The British are not coming to rescue me, or they would be here by now. And they wouldn't know what to do with Edith either.

So, times are hard, and I have to console myself, and Yvette and Maria when I have the strength, with the knowledge that I am giving my all for France.

I own a café which is being used by the Resistance for hiding two escaped airmen. It is dangerous, I know, but I insisted.

I still have to be nice to the Germans. They are my customers. Also, they are winning the war, despite my

efforts, and if I cross them they will shoot me. I care little
for myself, of course, but so many others depend on my
enormous support.

I have to be nice to my wife, because if she finds out
I'm having

with Yvette and sometimes
have to comfort Maria too, she will shoot me.*

Everyone seems to know about the airmen, except my
wife's mother, permanently bed-ridden in the attic – and
up to now I've had a better relationship with the Gestapo.
Edith knows about them. Leclerc, the ex-jailbird and
forger, knows about them. Even Colonel Von Strohm, the
Commandant of Nouvion, knows about them.

I worry about the Colonel – but fortunately I know his
secret. He and Captain Geering have concealed the
painting of The Fallen Madonna with the Big Boobies by
Van Clomp in a knockwurst sausage which is hanging in
my cellar. It is supposed to be a present for Hitler, but I
know they hope to sell it after the war.

I worry about Lieutenant Gruber. I know his secret as
well, only with that cologne he wears it's not much of a
secret.

I worry about Michelle of the Resistance. She keeps
popping out from behind the curtains in the back room
with a gun, just when the urge to perform my duty with
Yvette overwhelms me.

* It is difficult to tell why Edith has threatened René's life, especially
   since he is always ready to do his bit for France. Was she jealous of
   my mother? Very possibly. Yvette is referred to admiringly during the
   course of a great number of René's entries. Her desire for action in the
   most dangerous circumstances seems almost to have matched his own.

A terrible tragedy has occurred. Posterity has been denied an account of my incredible achievements for over a month!

I was in the cellar with Yvette, building a wall to conceal the painting of The Fallen Madonna with the Big Boobies by Van Clomp, and I accidentally hid my diary as well. We were disturbed by Edith just as I was putting the last brick in, and it must have slipped out of my trouser pocket.

I sometimes wonder whether I am the only hero of the Resistance in all France who takes the trouble to do a good job. Ah well, at least Yvette seems to appreciate it.

'You are the most exciting man I have ever laid with,' she said as we were nearly finished. How could I respond, in all modesty, and with a trowel full of wet cement in one hand? 'It is getting hard,' I said. 'And I must get it in immediately.'

I'm glad to say Edith understood why I had to wipe my filthy hands on Yvette's blouse, once I had explained the subterfuge. If Otto Flick of the Gestapo had caught me building a wall he would have been immediately suspicious.

I nipped down to the cellar yesterday evening to help Maria out, and found my priceless memoir in a very dark corner. My excitement was short-lived, but then that's often the way with Maria. All too soon Michelle of the Resistance appeared like a phantom out of the night with some disturbing news.

'She is in the back room,' Edith announced to me in front of a room full of German officers. 'Shall I sing a song to distract everyone?'

I told her it was not necessary. Although the singing of my wife is always very good for the sales of the cheese I can't help thinking that if it goes on we will start to lose customers.

Maria was at a table, attending to Lieutenant Gruber.

She must have been planning a quiet night in. 'I want you in the back,' I said.

'A little note would have been more discreet,' Gruber replied with that little smile of his that I find so alarming. Since his experiences on the Russian Front he's never quite lost the need for shared bodily warmth. The Russian Front was a very cold front. When I escaped with Maria to talk to Michelle, however, it suddenly seemed very appealing.

'I have information that you are to be interrogated by the Germans,' she said. 'They are ruthless men, and may even take your wife and torture her in front of you.'

What could I do but grit my teeth bravely. 'I will tell them nothing,' I said.

Michelle gave me a ring with a death pill in the clasp, in case I couldn't stand the pain. Then Colonel Von Strohm gave me a ring and told me to appear at his HQ immediately. Courageously, I told him that it would not be possible. I had to think of the café, the kitchen, my many responsibilities, and my bicycle which had a puncture. *Mon Dieu*, how I fought!

When he offered to send an armoured car, I put the phone down and ordered my walking boots and some sandwiches for the next morning's journey. The château requisitioned by the Germans wasn't far, but I thought I might take the scenic route.

6 FEBRUARY

Helga, the personal assistant of the Colonel, was very stern when she showed me in to his office yesterday. Some men like that, but I had more important things on my mind and a bottle of Château Lafite '37 in my pocket. Perhaps Helga thought it was meant for her.

But it wasn't. It was for Von Strohm, along with the cigars, a few cheeses and a Napoleon cognac I had cunningly brought as a diversion. For Helga, there was perfume.

It didn't work. No sooner had I handed over these gifts, than Captain Geering asked for a pair of pliers and a rubber hose. I won't say I wasn't appalled. I was. My whole life flashed before my eyes, and particularly the early days of my marriage to Edith. I may even have offered to tell them everything.

Thankfully, they just needed these things to mend the gas poker.

'René,' the Colonel spat, 'we know you are hiding two British airmen for the Resistance, and I am going to have you shot.'

Typically, I stood firm, and mentioned the painting of

The Fallen Madonna with the Big Boobies by Van Clomp
in my cellar. The Colonel was not made of such stern stuff.
He said he planned to hand the painting over to Otto Flick
of the Gestapo, so that they would leave him in peace. For
some reason he planned to hand me over as well. As a
gesture of friendship and respect he gave me a ring with a
death pill in the clasp.

'Perhaps you would like to give your wife one?'
suggested the Captain. I could see that my reputation
preceded me.

'Even a Frenchman cannot think of that sort of thing
at a time like this,' I said.

He felt it might provide the only way out. I thought I'd
try to find some others. I outlined a plan of great brilliance
and audacity. We would get Leclerc, the forger, to make a
copy of The Fallen Madonna with the Big Boobies. This
we would give to the Gestapo whilst keeping the original
to sell after the war. For his trouble, I had a hunch Leclerc
would accept little more than a Château Lafite '37, some
cigars, a Napoleon cognac and some perfume.

The cheese they could keep for my wife's next cabaret
performance.

On my return to the café I went instantly to the cellar
with Yvette. I resolved to keep the full details of my ordeal
from her. There are some things even a Frenchman will
not reveal in front of a woman.

'It was a nightmare. I never thought I would get out
alive.'

'Oh René,' Yvette breathed, 'you are so brave. When
you were there I lit candles.'

'You were praying for me?' I was touched, as I often
am by this innocent, vulnerable girl.

'We had a power cut.'

I'm glad to say everything was very soon turned on.

How near to disaster we heroes of the Resistance live in this world of cloak and dagger. I had planned to take a well-earned rest for a week or so – time to recuperate from my terrible experience at the château. But it was not to be. Scarcely had I removed The Fallen Madonna with the Big Boobies by Van Clomp from its resting place when the Gestapo arrived.

Even Edith's offer to sing privately to Otto Flick could not put him off. He had business to do, in the back room. And I knew that when he was finished with Helga, he would not be satisfied. It was a frightening thought.

I was trembling slightly as I showed Leclerc, the forger, the Madonna with the Big Boobies.

'Can you do another one?' I asked.

'You mean three Big Boobies?' the idiot replied, puzzled.

I made him aware of the gravity of the situation, but to no avail. He was prepared to attempt the artist's signature, but did not dare have a go at the boobies. I suppose he is rather old.

At that moment Maria announced that England was

calling on the radio concealed by Michelle of the Resistance in the bedroom of my wife's mother. I doubted that things could get worse, unless somebody lit a candle without first opening the window. The old bat eats nothing but onion soup.

The British airmen have been hiding in the cupboard by her bed, so although I cannot understand a word they say I expect they were as glad about the news from London as I was. A plane was coming to pick them up a week earlier than expected, and they had to leave immediately. Michelle of the Resistance confirmed this when she appeared like a phantom out of the night.

'Listen very carefully,' she said. 'I shall say this only once. The airmen must leave immediately.'

I was characteristically decisive. 'They cannot leave by the front; it is being watched. They cannot leave by the back; Herr Flick is having dinner there.' They couldn't leave by the window either, because the sheets from the bed of my wife's mother which we tied together didn't reach the ground.

Michelle was just quicker than me with the solution. 'They will have to leave disguised as Germans, in German uniforms.'

War is hell. I only knew one way we could get hold of them, especially at that time of night. 'I wouldn't ask this of you normally,' I said to dear, sweet Yvette. 'But you will be doing it for France!'

'I will be doing it for one hundred francs!' came the reply.

'And Maria?'

'She will do it for seventy-five.'

I'm sorry to say that the Colonel wasn't so accommodating. I explained that we only wanted to borrow their uniforms for about fifteen minutes, and that the airmen were taking the painting of The Fallen Madonna with the Big Boobies to England to have it copied. I mentioned that Yvette and Maria would be entertaining him and the Captain in the meantime with the flying helmet and the wet celery. I threw in the egg-whisk for good measure and Berlin suddenly seemed to them to be very far away.*

10 FEBRUARY

I woke up this morning to the news that the Colonel was not pleased with me, and was going to have me shot. Or he would have done if his gun hadn't been in its holster which was attached to a British airman who was escaping in his uniform. I was the first to hear this news because it was the Colonel who woke me up.

Still, I managed to look on the bright side. At least Lieutenant Gruber didn't wake me up. He admired my rings at the bar yesterday and showed me a little trinket of his own, a locket he wears round his neck. It had a picture inside.

'What beautiful, long, blonde hair,' I said.

'Yes, isn't it,' he sighed. 'Unfortunately he had to have it cut off when he joined the army.'

I can't help feeling he's not one of us.

The Colonel was even less pleased when I pushed him and the Captain into the cupboard in the bedroom of my wife's mother. What could I do? Herr Flick of the Gestapo was coming up the stairs and they had no clothes on. I told my wife's mother to say nothing to Herr Flick, if she knew what was good for her. She had obviously forgotten what was good for her, but then she is very old too.

'Good morning, Madam,' Flick said. 'I am sorry to put you to inconvenience, but there are certain things I wish to know.'

'There are two German officers in the wardrobe and

* One can only suppose from this exchange that René knows that food is the way to the Colonel's heart. Yvette and Maria are probably being asked to whip something up in the upstairs restaurant. I remain curious about this entry, though, because my mother was never a good cook. I can only imagine she was just that bit better than Maria.

CAFÉ RENÉ

A La Carte Menu
(Upstairs Only)

Appetisers

Tartes au Celeri Mouillé

(Tarts tantalisingly garnished with wet celery)

Petit Chou-fleur Farci au Nouvion

(Little cauliflower stuffed in the local way)

Soufflé avec Sauce du Chef

(A tasty dish, lightly whipped and served with the)

chef's favourite sauce)

Specialités du Maison

Saucisson Saupoudré avec des Epices

(A large knockwurst generously dusted with exotic spices)

Culotte de Boeuf René aux Flageolets

(Tender rump dressed by the chef. This mouth watering dish

cannot be beaten outside the Café)

Coq au Vin

(The wine is selected personally from the Café cellars, and

Captain Gearing tries his best to supply the coq)

Assortiment des Desserts

For those guests with a large appetite, may we

suggest something sweet on the trolley.

Prix Fixe / Service Compris

R

the radio is under my bed,' the old bat blurted. And she
has dared call me a coward.

'Very amusing,' Flick replied, 'I see I am wasting my
time here. *Heil Hitler!*'

I admit I was sweating a bit when I went down to help
Yvette and Maria with the chores. Yvette was desperate
to

me, so I told her to go into the
pantry and wait for me by the Brie. In the meantime I

Maria

and noticed that the velvet chaircover was
showing signs of wear.*

Just then, Yvette returned to say there was no Brie
and Michelle of the Resistance appeared with even worse
news. The two British airmen had been captured by the
Communist Resistance. So had the uniforms of the
Colonel and the Captain being worn by the airmen. And so
had The Fallen Madonna with the Big Boobies.

What were we to do? To get the Colonel and the Captain
out of the wardrobe in the bedroom of my wife's mother,
we had to get them uniforms. To get them uniforms, we
had to contact London, where they could be made. To
contact London, we had to use the radio in the bedroom of
my wife's mother. I didn't think the Colonel and the
Captain ought to know about the radio.

Unselfishly, I suggested that Michelle might be the
person to sort things out. We agreed that the
measurements for the uniforms would be sent to Savile
Row by carrier pigeon. At midday, Maria would go to a
secret address to pick up the pigeons. To avoid suspicion,
she would be disguised as a small boy.

'Why can I not be disguised as a small girl?' she asked.

---

* *Another tantalising gap in the text. My mother must have gone to the
pantry for a nibble, and was disappointed. But what of René and
Maria? Was the bravest man in France schooling the young waitress
in upholstery? He seems to think it was time to consider a little
stuffing.*

'Because you are a small girl,' Michelle explained reasonably.

11 FEBRUARY

Michelle of the Resistance found the location of the captured British airmen and Leclerc found Fanny again. Fanny, I discover, is the name of my wife's mother. They were childhood sweethearts and would have married had he not gone to prison. Given the choice, I think I would have done the same.

I led the expedition to rescue the airmen. It was nothing, really. My fellow heroes and heroines of the Resistance said anyone could have done it.

The Fallen Madonna with the Big Boobies is now back in safe hands. I wish I could say the same for the German uniforms. The foolish airmen burnt them when the communists took flight because they thought they would be shot as spies.

I might not tell the Colonel and Captain about this turn of events until tomorrow.

12 FEBRUARY

Or tomorrow.

13 FEBRUARY

Or the next day.

Hans's are red
The Colonels are blue
Goebbels hasn't got any
How about you?

14 Février

14 FEBRUARY

Valentine's Day!
I received just one card, unsigned, but perfumed with lily of the valley and a hint of diesel oil.
I sent only two. Both carried the same message.

My love is like a celery stick,
Divided into two.
My leaves I give to Edith,
But the stalk I give to you.

15 FEBRUARY

For the last few days Colonel Von Strohm and Captain Geering have been lurking in the café dressed as onion-sellers. These disguises were left in the wardrobe in the bedroom of my wife's mother by the escaping British airmen. And it is not even the onion season.

'Ah, Pierre, Jacques – the onion-sellers,' I greeted them as they sidled into the restaurant. 'Wine for my friends Pierre and Jacques. Sit down here, my friends.' Then, in a whisper, 'A brilliant disguise, my friends. We will get your uniforms as quickly as possible.'

'You said that yesterday, René,' said the Colonel.

'And the day before, and the day before that,' piped the Captain.

'If we don't get them today, you will be shot,' said the Colonel.

'Up against the wall, with guns,' piped the Captain.

I could tell that they weren't impressed, although even as these harsh threats were uttered I saw tears of compassion in their eyes.

'It is these damned onions,' said the Colonel, but he didn't fool me.

I moved to attend to my other customers as Maria came in with the basket of carrier pigeons, dressed as a small boy.* Thinking quickly, I welcomed her. 'Aha, little Georges, my nephew. It is good to see you, lad.'

'I have got what you want, Uncle,' she said, and I couldn't help noticing she had. Lieutenant Gruber, who was in his favourite position at the bar, noticed too.

'That boy is very well built, René,' he said with approval.

'Ah, it is my wife's cooking.'

'Why is he wearing stockings and suspenders?'

'We have many problems with him.'

---

* *This remains obscure. Why were the carrier pigeons dressed as a small boy?*

DUNGEON ROMEO GAVE Me BOILED EGG

ACHTUNG IT'S HELGA!

* 'Straighten up there, soldier, I like my troops erect!'

* Attention, boys! – it's Heart-breakin' Helga, hot from the

DER SUN SAYS:
STICK IT UP YOUR JUNKERS

...enly High-heeled Hip-hugger (36—24–36) — and rumour has it there's certainly a lot of lucky privates on parade up there!

★ But not to worry, boys — action-hungry Helga says she's gother eye on the Tank Corps for a posting soon …

★ Corps blimey, that's what we say! She can come and play with our helmets anytime!!

ALL THE
BESTEST
BOOBIES —
ONLY IN
DER SUN!

LE CAFE RENÉ

"Home of Café René – the finest Café in all France" proclaims the sign at the entrance to the quiet Normandy village of Nouvion, in the same quaint, rustic lettering that characterises Der Menu Touristisch in the Café window.

From the outside, the Café looks unremarkable enough, standing in the village square opposite the butcher with the big chopper. But is it indeed the finest Café in all France? Does le patron, René Artois, really deserve to be hailed – as he was by one recent anonymous contributor to this guide – as one of the great new stars of French cuisine and entertainment?

Certainly the menu is inventive, based on what Artois is determined to call his 'navel cuisine'. He prides himself, as chef, on his tasty tit bits. "The big hunk of meat is a thing of the past," he says, "unless the guest wishes to enjoy the delights of the more private dining room upstairs. There he will be able to enjoy everything from a little nibble to a grande bouffe in the French style."

It is in the philosophy of M. Le Patron as well as the dishes themselves that the true genius of Artois' creativity is displayed. Two contented diners, resplendent in their field grey uniforms, assured us that the waitresses are certainly generous with their portions, and though the service charge may appear a little steep, customers very seldom lost their shirts.

Wines have had to be decanted out of their bottles owing, in the words of Artois, to "agitation during a bombing raid." In the course of decanting they seem to have become a little on the thin side for the taste of our inspectors, but this is perhaps just a reflection of the choice of vintage. Artois also has his own-label cognacs, though these, too, seem to be from the same cru.

Artois himself cuts a noble figure as he walks around the Café in his white apron, chatting aimiably to customers. He is very much in the modern idiom of the working class hero, a man almost humbled by his own talent, resisting the lures of fame in favour of staying firmly in the saddle in Nouvion. René Artois is not a man to swan around opening supermarkets when he can be doing what he does best, inspecting the firmness of the melons in the larder, or kneading some dumplings in the kitchen.

Complaints from our correspondents are few, but one or two otherwise satisfied habitues of the Café would have welcomed a more extensive selection from the cheese board on cabaret nights.

I was wondering how the conversation was going to develop when Helga arrived with Herr Flick. The Gestapo officer went unerringly to the table of the Colonel and the Captain who were disguised as onion-sellers.

Herr Flick did not beat about the bush. 'Why are you dressed in the fashion of onion-sellers?'

'We can explain,' said the Colonel.

'He can explain,' piped the Captain.

'I am trying to infiltrate the Resistance,' said the Colonel. 'Dressed as a Colonel the French avoid me. With these I am one of them.'

At this Lieutenant Gruber forgot about the small boy with the stockings and suspenders. 'I am one of them too,' he said cheerfully.

After Herr Flick left to show Helga his private quarters, the Colonel returned to the subject of the uniforms. I tried to soothe him with the news that they were being made in London, by the finest tailors in Savile Row, but for some reason he became even angrier and decided that he was definitely going to hand me over to the Gestapo who would have me shot.

Once again I stared disaster in the face. There was only one thing for it. I reminded him that he had helped the British airmen to escape. I reminded him that he had stolen the priceless painting of The Fallen Madonna.

'René,' he said, 'I'm not sure you realise it, but this war is getting very dangerous.'

I reminded him of the flying helmet and the wet celery. That seemed to do the trick.

16 FEBRUARY

The airmen are back.

I had told Edith to do something unforgettable for the Colonel's lunch and was half-way through disciplining Maria about her stockings and suspenders when they appeared dressed as scarecrows at the back window. I

Duet for René and Edith

Composed by Roger and Leclerc

EDITH:
Outfits from Paris and nylons from Britain;
Letters from Alphonse that show how he's smitten:
Randy old suitors who want their last fling,
These are a few of my favourite things...

EDITH:
Boys in grey tunics with red shoulder flashes;
Chaps who own cafes with sexy moustaches;
Men who adore every note that I sing,
These are a few of my favourite things...

RENE:
Big balls of Edam and fingers of Gouda;
Soft runny goat's ones and some even ruder;
All kinds of cheese and the peace that it brings,
These are a few of my favourite things...

RENE:
When Leclerc plays,
When my wife sings,
When I'm feeling grim;
I simply remember my favourite cheese,
And then I don't hear a thing.

...dents are fe...
...e or two otherwis...
...lied habitues of the
...a.e would have wel-
comed a more extensive
selection from the
cheese board on
cabaret nights.

...d
...ured
...resses

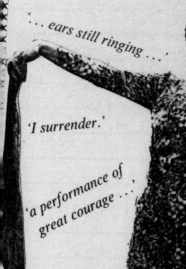

'A NIGHT TO REMEMBER'

The musical sensation of 1941 ...

The Sound of Edith
~ in Cabaret ~

'... ears still ringing ...'

WITH FULL SUPPORT!

'I surrender.'

'a performance of great courage ...'

'... never heard anything like it ...'

ADMISSION FREE!

don't know what they do for the crows but they scare the living daylights out of me. I have a terrible feeling that we are not going to get rid of these lunatics easily.

17 FEBRUARY

We communicated with London today, which is just as well since Edith casseroled the carrier pigeons for the Colonel's lunch. I was pleased to be able to tell our onion-sellers that their uniforms were being made by Solomon and Klein, the very finest tailors on Savile Row, and that they would be delivered by the RAF at dawn tomorrow.

The news wasn't greeted with quite the enthusiasm I anticipated. The Colonel was rather upset about the idea of wearing a Wehrmacht uniform with a Solomon and Klein label and the Captain was rather upset that he hadn't had the opportunity to order some extra shirts.

Edith was threatening to sing another song to tide us over this slightly difficult moment when Helga and Herr Flick entered the café, dressed as onion-sellers. I gathered from Helga later that the Gestapo officer had been very much impressed by the Colonel's plan to infiltrate the Resistance.

This he told her during a short period of casual interrogation yesterday afternooon. She seems to spend a lot of time in Herr Flick's soundproofed dungeon these days. Perhaps she is looking for ways of curing his limp a big softie*

and actually the soundproofing is to stop him being disturbed at night by the sound of heavy lorries.

---

* *I cannot be sure if Himmler himself censored this fascinating glimpse of a Gestapo officer on the job, or whether these two lines went the same route as the other missing parts of the diary.*
Interestingly enough, my mother says she never realised that Otto Flick had a limp. She just assumed it was the way he walked.

That's as maybe. As far as I'm concerned the Gestapo is the Gestapo is the Gestapo, especially when it calls Heinrich Himmler 'Uncle'. And even more especially when it has vowed to track down the hero of the Resistance who is hiding the painting of The Fallen Madonna with the Big Boobies by Van Clomp and have him shot.

Talking of which, I shall be very relieved when the RAF fly in at dawn tomorrow morning because they will be taking that too.

18 FEBRUARY

It is 3.00 am and I cannot sleep. It is often the case when we heroes of the Resistance are on the brink of action. I thought about arousing Maria and discussing my position by the icebox. Then I thought about discussing it in the cellar instead.

'But René,' I remember her saying to me once (or possibly twice), 'I get so dirty in there.'

She was right. And it is 3.00 am. I'm not sure I have the strength.

So here I am, dear Diary, to record the dramatic juggling act that I was called upon to perform yesterday evening. It is so difficult these days to keep all the Bols in

Yvette, Edith and Lt Gruber discuss René's bols

the air, especially when two of them are yours, and another is a bottle full of nitro-glycerine.

Let me explain.

I was in the process of asking Yvette to work with me under cover at around eleven o'clock tonight when Michelle of the Resistance appeared like a phantom out of the late afternoon.

'Now listen very carefully,' she said. 'I shall say this only once. You are to take this container and hide it in your cellar.'

'What does the container contain?' I asked.

'Bols,' she replied, brusquely.

I'm not easily offended, but I was a bit upset by her attitude, particularly since I have put myself between her and the enemy on so many occasions.

'No, no,' she said only once, unwrapping a bottle. 'Bols gin. This type of gin is coloured a very pale blue. Nitro-glycerine is also coloured a very pale blue. Be extremely gentle with it. Hide it in your cellar. At eleven o'clock there is going to be a big bang.'

I had to admit that her intelligence was impressive. 'I don't know what you are talking about,' I said.

'I will return quite soon to collect it. It is to blow up the railway line.'

All in all, it turned out to be a very explosive evening. Lieutenant Gruber spotted the bottle immediately, before I had a chance to put it in the cellar. He told me he was in the mood for something a little different. I thought about suggesting a girl, but he insisted on a Bols. I said that I didn't want to open a new bottle just to serve one drink.

'Very well, René,' he smiled that smile again, 'Two Bols. And perhaps you would like to give your wife one?'

This is obviously developing into a very popular German joke. 'Out of the question,' I said. But I still failed to avert catastrophe. Edith gave her mother a couple of glasses, and she blew the door off the cupboard in her room where the two British airmen are hiding again. They are having a terrible war. Even worse, Maria mixed some Bols with the chicken-feed to make them lay better. She said it always worked for her.

I'm sad to say that the poor things are now only good for stuffing pillows.

20 MARCH

Well, it has happened. Even the bravest man in France is not immortal. I know everybody warned me that it was on the cards, but it still took me by surprise. And what's more, it hurt. *Mon Dieu*, how it hurt!

I have been shot and killed.

And I'm too upset about it to write any more today.

21 MARCH

I must again plead your forgivenesss.* To recount to you the full, tragic story of the events leading up to my death may take many days, despite the fact that Yvette said yesterday evening that she would take dictation. I reluctantly declined her offer. Although her speed is as impressive as it ever was, my knees are still shaking.

22 MARCH

Forgive me, dear Diary. I'm still in a bit of a state. I have just been measured for my coffin by Monsieur Alfonse the undertaker, and my wife has chosen the most expensive oak casket with brass handles.

I may have recovered by tomorrow, but I doubt it.

* *It is typical of the author that although he had never intended this diary for publication, he maintains the most courteous and balanced tone towards his reader, even at a time of great personal distress.*

Today I am, after all, feeling a little calmer. To explain –
as we made our way through the early dawn to rendezvous
with the plane that was going to deliver the uniforms of
the Colonel and the Captain and pick up the two British
airmen and the one painting of The Fallen Madonna with
the two boobies (Leclerc never did get his hands on it) I
thought everything was going to be simple.

How wrong can one be?

This nightmare began over a month ago now, but it's
as if it were yesterday. Death plays strange tricks on a
man's memory.

There were apparently some things that Helga had not
revealed to us, though the Captain says not many. She
chose the night of the long Bols to reveal one that had
grave implications for every hero of the Resistance, and
especially me. General Von Klinkerhoffen was arriving at
ten o'clock the next morning for a thorough inspection of
all personnel.

It has to be said that the Colonel and the Captain were
not that pleased about it either. They were still dressed as
onion-sellers and their spare uniforms were in Berlin at
the de luxe cleaners. That is why they decided to join us.

When the Tiger Moth landed, everyone except the
British airmen noticed two things. The first was that it
was a Tiger Moth and therefore had only two seats,
including the pilot's. The second was that the Jewish tailor
who travelled as passenger had only been booked for one
appointment. He was happy to oblige with a fitting, but
was unwilling for some reason to stay with us until he had
finished the uniforms. As a result there was only room in
the plane when it left for The Fallen Madonna with the Big
Boobies, and even she took a bit of a squeeze.

I remained philosophical. The airmen were still with
us, and the Colonel and the Captain would get nice new
uniforms when General Von Klinkerhoffen sent them to
the Russian Front, except that they probably wouldn't

have Solomon and Klein labels. I resolved to return to *Le Café René* and make the best of things.

I hadn't realised that Michelle of the Resistance had immediate need of my heroism.

'Now listen very carefully,' she said before I had gone three paces. 'These are the orders for our next move. From here we go north.'

I've had more profitable orders. 'If you don't mind my saying, my café is south,' I explained patiently.

'The railway is north.'

'But we could walk home,' I said helpfully. 'Why take a train?'

'First we have to blow up the railway.'

That is when my real troubles began.

24 MARCH

'Hans,' the Colonel said to the Captain as the Tiger Moth disappeared into the distance, 'we are German officers. We are part of the great army that is winning the war. We do not blow up our own supply lines.'

'On the other hand,' the Captain piped, 'if we help them blow up the railway Von Klinkerhoffen's train will not arrive so we won't have to meet it so we won't need our uniforms so he won't find out we haven't got them.'

'And if you don't co-operate we will shoot you and hide your corpses in the copse.' I think it's fair to say that Michelle had the last word on the subject.

I led the heroic little band as it made its way gingerly through the undergrowth. I wasn't actually at the front, though, preferring instead to adopt a neat manœuvre

Lieutenant Gruber once told me he learnt at the Academy, which involved leading from the back.*

It seemed to work very well, except that I was closer to Yvette than I felt comfortable with. Every now and then a glimpse of her thigh reminded me that she had something very explosive concealed beneath her skirt. I suspect that she was as relieved as we all were to be able to unstrap the bottle of nitro-glycerine from her leg when we reached the cutting.

Michelle of the Resistance was worried that we might not have enough Bols to blow up the railway line, but the Captain proved that he had by throwing it by accident onto the track. I must say this surprised me. He's only a little fellow, and very short-sighted. I made a mental note to take this up with Maria.

I think it was then that the knockwurst really hit the fan. There was a huge explosion, and suddenly there were German soldiers everywhere. I fought bravely, as you would expect, but we were quickly overwhelmed. Surrender, alas, was the only answer.

As we were frogmarched to the cells, I thought not of myself. I thought of Edith wending her way sadly to the room of her mother with the news of my capture. And I thought of the smile on the old bat's face as she would say: 'You should have married the butcher. He like you. Every time you pass his shop he wave at you with his chopper.'

---

* *I initially assumed this to refer to the famed Military Academy at Heidelberg, but research has shown that the name of Hubert Gruber appeared only on the roll of the Dance Academy in Cologne.*

As we languished in the cells, even the Colonel reckoned the situation was serious, and he was the only person who could order our release. However, he could only do so by signing the papers in his office, and to do that he had to escape.

Helga thoughtfully provided a hacksaw to cut through the bars of the small window set high in the prison wall, and not so thoughtfully told us that General Von Klinkerhoffen was shortly to arrive by car. Apparently he was none too pleased about the railway track.

Since the Colonel could not fit through the small window, bars or no bars, I offered to try. This was not viewed favourably. I got the strong impression that if push came to shove the Colonel would tell the General that he thought the Captain might know something about the explosion. And the Captain would mention me.

I had a sudden image of them being taken away to Gestapo HQ for questioning, still carrying their onions. would cause quite a stink in Berlin. It was causing quite a stink where we were.

Yvette, of course, was a tower of strength. Maria, when she visited us to deliver another hacksaw blade, was the same, only smaller. They both wanted so much to place their bodies by my side if we were to be shot. I told them bravely that I'd rather they placed them in front, but there is a time and a place for everything.

Leclerc, the forger, came to pay his respects, disguised with his usual flair as a priest. He also delivered a hacksaw blade, along with the news that my wife and mother-in-law were coming to see me. Things were clearly going to get worse.

I thought the Captain had it bad; he now had three hacksaw blades hidden down his trousers. I would have taken them myself if I'd realised that no sooner were our visitors to appear than the Colonel and the Captain would escape, dressed in their clothes. It is the only time I have seen the Colonel grateful for his uncanny resemblance to my wife's mother.

Incarcerated then with those two women, death suddenly lost some of its sting. And when Edith told me she would sing the Marseillaise as the firing squad took aim, I hoped they would be quick on the trigger.

I must stop now. The very thought of Edith singing the Marseillaise drives me to the cognac bottle.

26 MARCH

I shall never forget being brought before General Von Klinkerhoffen in chains. The Germans obviously feared greatly that I was thinking of escaping to the hills, there to rally the forces of the Maquis behind me. They weren't far wrong.

The Colonel, to do him justice, said I should be released. He may have had The Fallen Madonna with the Big Boobies on his mind.

'I do not agree,' the General replied. 'We will shoot him as an example, tomorrow at dawn. Colonel, how does seven o'clock suit you?'

'Later would be better for me,' I said, even with Edith singing the Marseillaise. But it was not to be.

I faced the firing squad as the sun came up and bathed Lieutenant Gruber in its rosy glow. When he came closer

I realised he was wearing blusher. He was to command the squad.

'This is a very sad occasion for me, René.'

'I feel the same way, Lieutenant.'

'You French are so brave. Your mother-in-law has not one single tear.'

'This I believe,' I said. 'What about my wife?'

'She says she is going to sing the Marseillaise. Do you wish a blindfold?'

Earplugs would be better, I reflected. I could see Yvette and Maria in the distance, tears cascading down their cheeks. They must also have known what Edith had in store.

The squad raised their guns, took aim and fired. It was mercifully all over. Today was my funeral. It also went with a bang. Michelle of the Resistance had hidden some landmines in my coffin and it hit a tree.

Yvette and Maria cling to fond memories of René as they escort his coffin to its final resting place

27 MARCH

I should perhaps mention at this stage that the Colonel and the Captain had given the firing squad wooden bullets, which disintegrate three metres in front of the rifle. So I am not really dead, of course, though it still jolly well hurt. Only now I am managing to remove the last of the splinters with Yvette lending a hand.

The whole experience has had a very undesirable effect on me. Lieutenant Gruber has been kind enough to deny this, and so of course have Yvette and Maria. But I'm not the man I once was. The fact is, I have become my identical twin brother René, recently arrived from Nancy to run the café.

It was the Colonel's idea, and it seems to have worked. Herr Flick swallowed the story when Helga told him.

'After some interrogation,' she added.

The Colonel blanched. 'Why did he interrogate you?'

'It was raining, so we decided not to go out.'

With Lieutenant Gruber it was not so easy, but then it never is. And he was in charge of the firing squad.

'I hope you won't hold it against me,' he said.

I assured him I wouldn't.

'You bear a most remarkably close resemblance to your late brother. You even have the same pretty rings. But now I come to look, your eyelashes are a little longer and your hands seem more artistic.'

It was a very bad sign, now that I was a single man, and from Nancy into the bargain.

Otherwise little has changed. The two British airmen have moved from the bedroom of my wife's mother to the henhouse, where they are probably disguised as turkeys. Roger Leclerc has moved from the cellar to the bed of my wife's mother, where he is disguised as a complete idiot. They are all very convincing disguises. I wish I felt better about my own.

Today it was the Colonel's birthday. He wouldn't say which, though Yvette tells me he is in some ways still remarkably youthful. I baked him a cake. The icing was plaster of Paris because the Captain failed to supply the sugar, but the candles were real.

'In France,' I told him, 'it is the tradition that they must be blown out by one big puff.'

'It is your birthday, Colonel,' Lieutenant Gruber said generously.

Yvette had a surprise for him in her bedroom at nine o'clock this evening. Maria had a surprise for him at eight. All in all it made me rather look forward to my next birthday. Until Edith announced that she would surprise him too, with a special song.

'Your wife has many talents, René,' piped the Captain when Edith had finished.

'A pity they do not include singing,' the Colonel said. I had to agree. Edith could not carry a tune in a bucket.

'A little champagne, Colonel,' I said. After my ordeal, I was in an expansive mood.

'With champagne glasses!' He was delighted to see what Maria was carrying.

'Of course. And I will tell you a legend. It is said that these glasses were modelled on the bosom of Marie Antoinette.'

'They should have been modelled on Helga's bosom,' piped the Captain, 'we'd have got a bigger drink.'

'There is also a legend about where they got the idea for the champagne cork,' Lieutenant Gruber said.

'Let us talk no longer of the past.' The Colonel spoke for all of us. 'Let there be wine, women –'

'And song!' Edith cried joyously.

'No!' said the Colonel. 'Just wine and women.'

It is really very sad that just as they were starting to enjoy themselves, the Captain and the Colonel were seized by the girls of the Communist Resistance and taken away

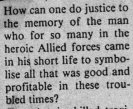

THE TIMES

How can one do justice to the memory of the man who for so many in the heroic Allied forces came in his short life to symbolise all that was good and profitable in these troubled times?

Rene Artois, killed tragically in action, will undoubtedly be in line for the highest award for gallantry it is in His Majesty's power to bestow.

He is survived by his widow, Edith, and is mourned by his many friends.

Colonel Artois (though he was too modest to use his rank) spent much of the war undercover, but his exploits have become legendary. Attractive, courageous, vita

DIE WELT

How can one do justice to the memory of the man who for so many heroes of the Wehrmacht (and the SS) came in his short life to symbolise all that was good and profitable in these troubled times?

Rene Artois, executed as a result of a tragic administrative blunder, should undoubtedly be in line for the highest award for gallantry it is in the Fuhrer's power to bestow.

He is survived by his widow, Edith, and is mourned by his many friends in the Wehrmacht (and the SS).

Rene Artois spent much of the war undercover, looking for the Fallen Madonna with the Big Boobies by Van Klomp, which he always meant to give the Fuhrer for his birthday. He

FRANCE SOIR

How can one do justice to the memory of the man who for so many heroes of the Resistance came in his short life to symbolise all that was good and profitable in these troubled times?

Rene Artois, killed tragically in action, will undoubtedly be in line for the highest award for gallantry it is in General De Gaulle's power to bestow.

He is survived by his widow, Edith, and is mourned by his many friends.

Colonel Artois (though he was too modest to use his rank) spent much of the war undercover, but his exploits have become legendary. Attractive, courageous, vital, he

Even in the midst of war the national and international press were quick to print eulogies of the man who for so many had come to symbolise all that was good and profitable in these difficult times.

The unenviable task of summing up the many virtues and achievements in the life of Rene Artois fell, not surprisingly, to his twin brother, Rene Artois.

to be shot. Their crime? Ordering my own execution only a few short days before.

I must admit that the irony was not lost on me. Nor was the fact that I might not have to share the painting of The Fallen Madonna with the Big Boobies by Van Clomp. Call me a hero, call me a sentimental fool, but I have always felt strongly that they should remain in the hands of a Frenchman.

29 MARCH

I couldn't sleep a wink last night. Yvette and Maria were almost inconsolable, and naturally, because they served under me, I had to attend to them. Yvette, as always, was worried that her poor, crippled mother would not survive without the food parcels and paraffin she had persuaded the Colonel to supply.* Maria was just worried that her own appetite would not be satisfied, and I must say this morning so am I.

Breakfast was a sorry affair. We were all extremely upset that there was no butter, very little sugar, and only one cup of coffee that I felt compelled to drink personally to keep morale up. I began to realise that we might have to rescue these Germans, for the good of France.

* It is a great tribute to my mother's self-sacrifice that my maternal grandmother lived to the age of 103, and was by all accounts entertaining her friends in a very energetic fashion right up to her death.

30 MARCH

Michelle of the Resistance appeared this evening, like a phantom out of the wardrobe in the back room. It is less than two days since the Colonel and the Captain were kidnapped, but already their absence has been noticed. Herr Flick was on his way to the café at that very moment.

'Listen very carefully, I shall say this only once,' she said. 'The Gestapo will investigate the disappearance of the Colonel and if they find the transmitter and the codebook you will all have had your chips.'

We acted with characteristic speed. Michelle threw the radio out of the window of the room of my wife's mother onto a passing truck whilst I fed the book-page by page to the two British airmen. I think they would have preferred to eat something hot, but they had to make do with code.

Flick interrogated us all closely, and it wasn't as much fun as Helga keeps implying. Lieutenant Gruber was especially worried that the Gestapo would discover that he was bending over behind the bar at the time of the abduction.

'You!' Flick barked. 'Did you see the face of the kidnapper?'

'She was just an ordinary French girl,' Gruber replied uncomfortably.

'Would you recognise her?'

'All girls look the same to me.'

Flick responded by telling him to round up ten peasants and shoot them in the town square if the Colonel and the Captain were not found. That decided me. That, and the fact that I hadn't even had a cup of coffee for breakfast that morning.

31 MARCH

I would have gone alone, but in the event two girls from the Communist Resistance pounced on me late last night when I was putting the cat out. I assumed they were acquainted with my reputation, but they were only there to escort me to the lonely barn where the Colonel and the Captain were imprisoned. I was glad of their company, particularly since I was blindfolded.

'You are the brother of the man who was shot,' the leader of the band told me when I arrived. 'You are to have the honour of shooting the men who have raped France.'

It is true that these men were our enemies, though I felt the use of the word 'rape' was a little strong. Maria for one had always seemed most obliging. How was I to explain to these courageous but naive women that for René Artois things were not so straightforward? Their war was a series of small-scale raids, whilst I was in control of the big picture. Or would be as soon as the RAF delivered it.

Although every fibre of my being cried out against it, I resolved to deceive them. 'I would like to savour the moment of revenge alone.'

I had just had time to chastise the Colonel for getting us into this mess when the Resistance band returned. They had intercepted an RAF parachute drop whose contents they found baffling: two German uniforms tailored in Savile Row and two identical paintings by Van Clomp. They dropped everything when shots were suddenly fired outside. They must have been very frightened.

Our rescuers were Michelle, Yvette, Maria and Edith,

dressed in German uniforms. My wife was wearing the jackboots, but the mission was Michelle's idea. There is clearly no limit to her desire to have me as leader of our heroic group.

We greeted each other with fond embraces, as is the French custom, and I shook hands warmly with Edith before making my way back to the café.

I was just putting the finishing touches to this entry and Yvette was complimenting me on my style when we were aroused by banging downstairs. The Colonel and the Captain had come to deliver the painting of the Fallen Madonna, and the news that Herr Flick was in possession of the forgery.

1 APRIL

April Fool's Day – but when I told the Colonel and the Captain early this morning that they had given the original to Herr Flick and kept the forgery by mistake, I wasn't joking.

When they said that unless I got the real one back before it was sent to the Fuhrer in Berlin I would be shot, they weren't either.

I felt at last that everything was returning to normal.

2 APRIL

Maria and I were in the pantry having a little nibble at the Brie when Michelle of the Resistance called to tell me that the new radio transmitter was being delivered today by that old fool Leclerc, disguised as a cheese salesman.

'He will be the bearer of a suitcase containing cheese,' she said only once.

'How will he carry the radio?' I asked.

'He has a false bottom.'

I wondered why in that case he needed the suitcase. I

also wondered what we would do with the extra cheese. The only answer was to ask Edith to do a special Gala Cabaret Night.

I'm afraid that I only have the strength for a short entry today because my wife interrupted a bout of hand-to-hand combat I was having with Yvette in the back room. The only way of convincing her that I was teaching our waitresses self-defence was by asking Yvette to demonstrate on me how she would fight off the drunken overtures of a German soldier. Unfortunately, she did.

3 APRIL

Bad news from the Colonel, especially for a man with a hernia. Herr Flick of the Gestapo is putting the painting of the Fallen Madonna with the Big Boobies on the train to Berlin tomorrow at mid-day. Hitler has told Himmler to pick it up personally.

'Here is what we do, René,' he said. 'By my orders tonight you will close your café for my private party to celebrate the anniversary of the burning down of the Reichstag. Helga here will give Herr Flick information about the party and tell him that he is not invited.'

'I only have to hint and he will drag it out of me,' she said.

'This will arouse his suspicions and he will not be able to stay away. While Herr Flick is enjoying himself with the girls dressed as Hitler Youths, you will be at his private quarters switching the paintings.'

Somehow I knew there was going to be a catch. I wanted nothing to do with Herr Flick's private quarters. It was very dangerous to mess with the Gestapo.

With my usual generosity, I offered to give the party instead.

Just then that old fool Leclerc delivered the new radio concealed in a Dutch Edam. It was never my favourite cheese, and went down further in my estimation when it crackled into life whilst I still had it behind the bar.

'Listen carefully,' it said, 'I will meet you behind the woodshed at one o'clock.'

I later discovered from the new code book that I was being told to take the two British airmen to the coast tonight. Unfortunately Lieutenant Gruber got the impression that I was inviting him to share some intimate memories of my boyhood in Nancy.

'See you later then,' he said gaily.

It was turning into quite an evening.

I left the party before it had even started. Lieutenant Gruber was at the piano, singing *Falling in Love Again*. It never fails to bring tears to my eyes, and certainly didn't then.

We made our way courageously to the château. I was dressed in the Savile Row uniform of the Colonel and Edith was in the Captain's, but again she wore the jackboots.

I regret now that I was generous enough to let her take charge. I feel sure that if the pillow with which I was bulking out the uniform of the Colonel had not started to slip towards my crutch, I would not be in the position I am now – back at the café having left the copy of the painting of the Fallen Madonna with the Big Boobies in Herr Flick's room, and without repossessing the original.

And what Lieutenant Gruber is going to make of the pillow when I get to the woodshed I dread to think.

4 APRIL

I backed out of our meeting in the woodshed. It seemed the only way. Lieutenant Gruber was upset, of course, but consoled himself with a little pirouette or two on the dance floor.

The party was a great success, judging by the state of the restaurant this morning. The only shorts left behind the bar belonged to the girls dressed in the uniform of the Hitler Youth.

Taking the two British airmen to the beach to pick up their boat home was not so much fun. It wasn't until we got there that Michelle discovered that one of them got seasick even on the boating lake of Regent's Park.*

As we headed back to the café with them, I wasn't pleased. I had led our brave little group through the coastal defences at great personal risk. We had disguised ourselves by then as Hitler Youths, and my trousers were very tight.

Yvette, at least, was as supportive as always. 'René, I feel tonight that the years have fallen away from you,' she said. 'You sound much younger too.'

I was doubly glad that Lieutenant Gruber was not waiting in the woodshed.

12 APRIL

It has been more than a week since I put pen to paper. This is because it has been a very slow week for business. I've needed both hands, as well as the help of my staff, to massage some feeling back into my lower limbs. With uniforms that tight, I'm amazed the Hitler Youth haven't lost more of their members.

The British airmen have been hidden in the nearby nunnery. For a while I thought it might be all I was good for as well.

I discovered this morning that Herr Flick also had made a forgery of the painting of the Fallen Madonna with the Big Boobies by Van Clomp. He now has not two but six boobies in his hands. And that's not including Helga.

* *This sounds very much like my stepfather.*

13 APRIL

There has been a lot of banging here recently, but it is only my demented widow in the back room looking for my will, which leaves everything I possess to her.

She can bang all day. It is hidden in a compartment behind the cuckoo clock where she will never find it.

14 APRIL

She has found it.

I was taking a drink rather gingerly with Lieutenant Gruber when the cuckoo gave a strangled cry and my secret was out.

'"I do hereby leave all of which I stand possessed,"' Edith read triumphantly, '"to my dear and faithful wife, who has comforted me and filled me with joy during the happy days of my marriage."'

'The nights were a different story,' I muttered.

'There is something written on the back,' Yvette said.

'"P.S. To Yvette ..."' Edith read. 'I can hardly read it. It is as if his hands were shaking.'

'He must have been getting on a bit by then,' I said.

'No, I've got it. "To Yvette, who has served so devotedly under me, I leave the collapsible sofa in the parlour."' Edith's brow furrowed. 'That sofa is not collapsible.'

'It is unless you put a book under it,' Yvette said

brightly.

'"P.P.S.,"' Edith continued. '"To Maria, I leave the small billiard table which has given us both so many moments of pleasure."'

I have to admit that I've had some lucky breaks on that table.

'Dear René,' Lieutenant Gruber said wistfully. 'He was a good man. There was something soft and sensitive about him.'

'I know how he felt,' I said.

15 APRIL

Since my death, life has not been bleaker. For a whole day now my widow has been helping herself to my estate. My best cognac, the cash out of the till, all the things a Frenchman holds sacred are now technically hers.

Well, not quite all. I must admit that I am gaining considerable pleasure from the fact that both Yvette and Maria are already putting my bequests to them to immediate good use.*

---

* *I can confirm everything the great man says. The collapsible sofa still has pride of place in our parlour all these years later. I often return from the office to discover my mother putting her feet up on it.*

   As for the billiard table, she tells me that Maria left it behind when she mailed herself to Switzerland, but not before considerably improving her technique.

Odes to a Nancy Boy

War Poem
If I should cry think only this of me.
That there was some corner of the Russian
front
That was very, very cold.

Ode to René's own Label Cogna
They shall not grow old, as we
that are left grow old
Age shall not weary them, nor the
years condemn.
As the going down of the bottle and in
the morning
We will remember them, even if you
forget where you put the label.

16 APRIL

I'm under a great deal of pressure.

My widow is spending all my money attempting to attract a new suitor. She is parading herself around Nouvion in a new hat which looks like a dead hen, trying to lure a rival café-owner into her grasp. The mother of my widow rubs salt into my wounds by adding that he has a bigger one than me. That's definitely the last time I wear the uniform of the Hitler Youth.

The Colonel is being equally harsh. He is threatening to have me shot again unless I give him the names of my Resistance group.

'But Colonel,' I say courageously, 'I do not know their names. They are mostly girls, and only reveal themselves at night.'

'I wish to get my hands on them,' said the Colonel.

'Me too,' piped the Captain.

It took all my powers of inventiveness to divert their line of questioning, and quite a lot of wet celery.

'And the flying helmet,' said the Colonel.

'And the flying helmet,' I agreed.*

'And a great big steaming plate of spaghetti bolognese and three feet of elastic,' piped the Captain.

We were both speechless for a moment.

'Hans,' said the Colonel slowly, 'Just between the two of us, what exactly have you got in mind?'

'I thought I would have a quick snack while Maria repairs my long winter underwear.'

17 APRIL

Hubert Gruber and I are getting to know each other much better these days. I'm not convinced it is a good idea, but it is for France.

He told me today that Herr Flick had a compromising

* *There are many references to the flying helmet throughout the text. I can only assume that the Colonel was preparing to perform some fairly complex aerobatic manœuvres.*

photograph of him and, worst of all, with a woman. 'My commanding officer will never forgive me, René,' he said, 'and I'm most concerned that this will change *our* relationship.'

I assured him it wouldn't.

Apparently Flick will reveal the photograph if Hubert tells anybody about his recent glimpse of the Gestapo officer's private quarters.

'Flick has three Fallen Madonnas with Big Boobies, René. One is a forgery he commissioned himself, one arrived mysteriously at his HQ, and one is genuine. A peasant was clearing his room and mixed them up.'

'How do you know all this?' I said, feigning disinterest.

'I was taken there in a sack.'

'How dreadful,' I said.

'Actually, I found it rather exciting. The soldier who carried the sack had very broad shoulders.'

'But why?'

'I expect he takes a lot of exercise.'

'No,' I said. 'Why did Herr Flick want to see you?'

'He knew I had artistic leanings.'

'But I thought he was interrogating Helga pretty much full time these days,' I said, baffled.

'Yes,' Hubert replied. 'He only wanted me to tell him which was the real painting. I was able to identify one as a genuine early Van Clomp.'

I asked him how.

'When he was taller he signed his paintings further up.'

18 APRIL

The Colonel was very anxious about Lieutenant Gruber's visit to Gestapo HQ. He interrupted me during a special service I was holding for myself in the back room. It was the only way I could account for the presence of the two British airmen, who have returned dressed as nuns, though I did think of saying we were collecting for my organ fund.

'René,' the Colonel said, 'does Lieutenant Gruber know anything?'

'René has always been very careful not to drop anything in front of him,' Yvette said.

'I find the presence of nuns very uplifting,' the Captain piped.

'In that case,' the Colonel said, 'we must go.'

19 APRIL

Edith, apparently, has been putting herself about a bit. It can't have been with the Germans, or they would have surrendered immediately.

'I am so proud of her,' said the mother of my widow. 'They were round her like flies.'

'I expect her hat has gone off,' I said.

Beneath this jovial exterior, however, lies a very worried hero of the Resistance. I'm not frightened of the Gestapo. I'm not frightened of being shot again. But my widow scares out of me the living daylights. She is spending my money like water. And the worst thing of all is that if I want to get my restaurant back, I may even have to marry the old bat all over again.

Michelle of the Resistance provides the only spark of hope. She will return imminently to collect the two British airmen. I find I admire her and more and more, having seen her in action. I wonder if she would ever

with me. Perhaps, but probably only once.*

* *Michelle seems regularly to have followed René's lead during this period, so this reference remains confusing. It is possible that the missing section of the journal would reveal what was on his mind.*

Helga tells me Herr Flick opened his raincoat to her in the Colonel's office yesterday evening to reveal something of enormity to her. An unusually large knockwurst, emblazoned with a little swastika.

In it, he explained, was the real painting of The Fallen Madonna by Van Clomp, which he wants me to hide in my kitchen. He has another containing the forgery he wishes the Colonel to send to the Fuhrer in Berlin.

The third painting he found too hot to handle, so destroyed it in a very large furnace. It seems everything is too hot to handle these days. Now that I am a single man, Yvette and Maria both

explosive, hidden in the broom cupboard.* And what's more, Hubert Gruber has presented me with a little luxury gift from Gay Paris. A charming cologne, very popular with the tank corps: lily of the valley, with a hint of diesel oil.

---

* *Yet again we glimpse our hero at the centre of affairs. It is extraordinary that anything so likely to blow up in his face should be hidden in the broom cupboard, but it is another sign of René's bravery. Besides, he had probably tried everywhere else.*

Maria goes weak at the knees when René shows her the whereabouts of something explosive

21 APRIL

Helga has concocted a plan of such audacity that only I can carry it out. Unknown, of course, to Herr Flick, we are going to send the Fuhrer a forged knockwurst containing no painting. The real knockwurst containing the forged painting will be stamped with a forged swastika and hung in my kitchen. The real knockwurst with the real painting stamped with the real swastika will be hidden in my cellar and sold after the war.

I have to cook the forged knockwurst, which will then be put on a train to Berlin. I am to tell my fellow heroes of the Resistance that there are valuable secret military supplies on the train and they will blow it up. If I don't, I will be shot.

Leclerc (for it is he)
delivers the knockwurst

Oh well, I suppose it will save me from having to woo Edith for a while. At least for the twenty-two-and-a-half minutes it will take to cook the knockwurst.

22 APRIL

Leclerc, the forger, arrived yesterday evening disguised as a simple village idiot. I congratulated him on his most convincing role yet.

'You will rendezvous at the cowshed of Farmer Claude at one o'clock tonight,' he said. Luckily he said it only once because manure formed a large part of his cover, and the smell was beginning to get to me.

'I won't,' I replied.

For some reason, Edith, who was eavesdropping on my briefing, jumped to the conclusion that I, who had died for France once already this year, was a coward. And a coward she could not marry.

We were there at a quarter to. The airmen were already in the shed, waiting to be milked. They were dressed as a pantomime cow. Disguised as a mushroom picker, I had to lead them and five other cows across a road heavily

BRITISH ONTELLIGENCE HEADQUITTERS

Curse Repote: *Crabtree*

This curse lasted for six whacks, and dolt with all aspics of longwodge and disgeese. Successful gradiots will be folly trooned to piss as a native, moaning, noon and nit.

Disgees: *God*

Escape plons: *God*

Longwodge: Very god—farty out of fifty. His French cod not be butter.

Roodio: *Spook well.*

Massage from the headmooster: This gradiot pissed out with tap marks for fartitude. He is complotely fat to go aboot the bosness of a French poloceman. God lick!

guarded by Germans. Edith was behind me with a gun.

It was not my lucky night. The plane arrived on time, but did not land. Instead it dropped the packages by parachute. One was an escape package for the two airmen; the other was another British idiot who speaks French like my widow cooks.

Then one of the cows dropped another two packages on my foot.

After much concentration and some help from Yvette, I learn that the new man is saying his name is Crabtree and that he is a secret intelligence officer, which is why he is disguised as a gendarme. Judging from his performance so far, he keeps his intelligence very secret indeed.

Before leading the pantomime cow back to Farmer Claude's, I outlined to Michelle my audacious plan to blow up the Berlin train. Not for the first time since she has been under my command, she asked me to listen very carefully.

'No,' she said.

Not for the first time, I got the feeling that I might have to get on the job myself.

24 APRIL

Sure enough, this very evening I found myself in the turret of Lieutenant Gruber's little tank, with the Captain at the wheel.

The plan was very simple. We were to make our way to the railway track, fire one of the Lieutenant's twenty-millimetre shells at the ammunition truck of the Berlin Express, thereby destroying both the train and the forged knockwurst, and return before the Lieutenant and the Colonel finished dinner. It was Helga's plan. I'm beginning to think there is more to her than meets the eye.

I can't claim that the mission was a complete success.

When we headed home half an hour later, we had blown up one signal box, destroyed the Colonel's car and lost the cologne and ladies' underwear from the Lieutenant's glove box. Unfortunately we left the train – and the forged knockwurst – intact.

An hour later, we had been shot at by the Resistance, foiled Michelle's plan to blow up an ammunition lorry, and watched Otto Flick blow up his own staff car.

'And worst of all,' Lieutenant Gruber wailed, 'there are nasty little dents all over my little tank and the wheels are covered in mud.'

Lt Gruber shows off his little tank

25 APRIL

This morning the Colonel and the Captain were good enough to drop in at the café on their way to Switzerland. They didn't want to wait and see how the Fuhrer was going to react to their present of an empty knockwurst.

It was going to take a special kind of courage to make that journey; dressed as Frenchmen, carrying little more than the week's payroll for the garrison and the original painting of the Fallen Madonna with the Big Boobies by Van Clomp. For a moment, I was tempted to go with them.

We were sharing a last cognac when that stupid fool Crabtree came in.

'I have good nose,' he said.

'Yes, you are very handsome,' I replied. 'Now go away.'

'The troon carrying the sausage was bummed by the RAF.'

'Bummed by the RAF?' I said.

'Bummed by the RAF?' Lieutenant Gruber asked, forgetting for a moment about his armoured car.

'I think he means bombed,' I said, wishing to let Hubert down gently.

'Yes, in a grote big poof –' Crabtree said.

'– of smoke, Hubert, of smoke,' I said.

'What a pity,' the Colonel beamed. 'I think that calls for a drink.'

26 APRIL

My widow is continuing to dress herself up like the dinner of a dog and parade around the town square in search of suitors. It is beginning to worry me. Not half as much as it should worry them, but that is little consolation.

Yvette, on the other hand, is a lot of consolation. I took her in the back-room this afternoon

collapsible sofa.

Unfortunately, I was more exhausted than I realised by the previous night's activities so   my will and left it to her.*

At that moment, Michelle of the Resistance and the stupid fool Crabtree climbed in through the window.

'The escape package brought by this British agent was damaged in the landing. You must help to mend it,' Michelle said.

'Mend it?' I replied. 'I don't even know what it is.'

'It is a balloon made of silk. Filled with hot air, it will lift the airmen in the basket and, with a favourable wind, take them back across the channel.'

'If you want an unfavourable wind, you could take the mother of my widow as well.' I suddenly felt much more cheerful.

'But some of the fabric is torn away and missing. We will need silk to replace it,' Michelle said.

'You must go and get your hands on girls' knockers,' Crabtree announced. For a moment, I began to think he wasn't as stupid as he looked.

---

*   Another mention of the collapsible sofa. It is obviously a piece of some value, and René was making absolutely sure that his will would be followed to the letter.

My Dear Madame Edith

Please marry me. I am a man of substance. I have my mortuary, a butcher's shop, the lease of the barbers and five thousand shares in Volkswagen. Whichever way the war goes, you will be provided for.

Your loving undertaker with the twenty-four hour service

Alphonse

'He means knickers,' Michelle said.

'Even better,' said I. Perhaps we could start by asking Yvette. She would probably give me one for France, or even better, a pair. I resolved to get on the job immediately.

27 APRIL

Nouvion is witnessing signs of patriotism that must do every Frenchman's heart proud. All the girls in the Resistance have sacrificed their knickers, and as far as I have been able to ascertain, with very little hesitation.

28 APRIL

Yvette, spurred on no doubt by the example of her companions, has now given up her entire supply.* It is very satisfying.

29 APRIL

Just when I thought things were finally going my way, Edith has to ruin it. I found her entertaining a suitor in the restaurant today, and he was very familiar.

'Monsieur Alfonse has come to ask for my hand in marriage,' she said.

'But what has an old undertaker got to offer?' I asked.

At this, he took out a list. 'I have, as you know, my own establishment. Since the war, business has been very brisk. I have two hearses and four horses. I have in stock twenty-six ready-made coffins. I have seventy-two metres of planed oak, stocks of elm and pine, twenty-six marble angels, twelve concrete cherubs, fifty kilos of assorted

---

* My mother is still like that. 'René,' she would say to me as I grew up, 'charity begins at home.'

handles and twenty-six litres of embalming fluid.'

'Oh René,' said Maria as she poured Monsieur Alfonse another cognac, 'how romantic!' I wondered why he had to come to my café to get pickled.

'I should mention that I also have a small hearse with a smaller horse –'

'Very handy for shopping,' I said.

'– I live in a luxury apartment above the mortuary and I aim one day to have a little crematorium of my own.'

'Well, Edith,' I said, 'at least if you get taken suddenly in the night, you won't have far to go.' What I didn't say was that if the early days of our marriage were anything to go by, it would be Monsieur Alfonse who would end up on the slab.

30 APRIL

I must admit that the undertaker has left us with plenty to ponder upon, as well as more than a faint smell of embalming fluid. I found myself thinking wistfully of Hubert's cologne. But not that wistfully.

I found myself also thinking that Edith's offer to keep me on as barman when she married Monsieur Alfonse was too much to take lying down. I went to ask Yvette for her advice.

1 MAY

The back room is covered with silk knickers. I haven't seen such a sight since the Nouvion Rangers came to the café to celebrate winning the cup in '38. I remember their Captain telling me they had never had such a good score. Yvette, Maria and Michelle of the Resistance are hard at it, sewing them all together to mend the balloon.

That old fool Leclerc, the forger, is still doing his bit. He came back this afternoon with a pair big enough to make a whole new balloon.

'This was my finest hour,' he said.

I'll admit I was surprised. It looked like at least an hour and a half.

Unfortunately one of our group must have overstepped his brief. Helga reported to the Colonel – and worse still, the Gestapo – that her own knickers had been removed in the garden, when she was not even looking. The red ones, with the little swastikas embroidered on the edge. Not that I had ever seen them.

The Colonel was despatched to the café to track down the culprit. I was trapped. There was only one way out. I did it for France.

'Colonel,' I said, 'it is very simple. We need silk, which is in very short supply, to make a wedding dress.'

'A wedding dress?' he said. 'How romantic! Who is it for?'

'For me,' I replied. 'I am to be married to Edith.'

There were a lot of tears, of course, for it was a very emotional moment. Lieutenant Gruber took it particularly hard, and so did Yvette and Maria.

I'm sad to say that Monsieur Alfonse took it hardest of all. 'Monsieur,' he said coldly, 'you have humiliated me. You have insulted me. I demand satisfaction.'

'I don't suppose you'd settle for the flying helmet and the egg-whisk, would you?' I said hopefully.

His response was to slap me with his glove and hand me his card. 'Swiftly and with style,' it proclaimed. I had a nasty feeling he was looking for business.

CAFÉ RENÉ

My dear Friends in Avignon

Pity a poor old woman who is haunted by an undertaker
who keeps coming to pay his respects.
"Dear Madame Fanny," he said to me today, "I bring flowers to the
beautiful lady who may, pray God, soon be my mother-in-law."

The Communists have René and he is on their hit-list. He
may already have kicked the bucket. Still, better dead than red.
But in anticipation, Alfonse is asking for my daughter's hand.
What would become of me?
"There is a granny annexe over the mortuary."
"Permission not granted."
I held out for a cottage with roses round the door, a personal servant
and a handsome chauffeur to push my wheelchair. Alfonse agreed
to my terms. He said we will lay the first brick the day the war is over.
"Not likely," I said. "The foundations must be laid immediately after
the wedding."

Don't you agree, my dear Friends, getting laid after the war
will be no good to me.

Please write soon and enclose a little food if you can - this gruel makes
a terrible smell in my bedroom.

Your poor old friend

Fanny

R

I have spent much of the last twenty-four hours hiding in the hen-house, and I must admit I feel like a bit of a turkey. I just can't help thinking that it would be a terrible waste if a hero of the Resistance were to have his life cut short by the bullet of an ancient undertaker. Especially since I have already been shot once this year.

I realise now that despite my more or less perpetual acts of heroism for my country, I am a man who detests violence.

The cockerel was starting to give me a very strange look when I heard someone outside.

'René, it is I, Yvette. You may reveal yourself.'

Normally I would have done. But I didn't want to give the cockerel the wrong idea.

'What is happening?' I said.

'Lieutenant Gruber has accepted Monsieur Alfonse's challenge on your behalf. He defended your reputation. They were saying you have a yellow streak.'

So would they have, I thought, if they had been sitting all night on half a dozen eggs.

I returned to the café to hear Edith addressing the Colonel, the Captain and Lieutenant Gruber. 'I am most grateful to you,' she said, 'for upholding the honour of my future husband who scarpered out of the scullery window when those men arrived.'

'I'm sure René would not run away like a coward,' Hubert said. 'There will be an explanation.'

'Of course there will,' the Colonel said.

And of course there was, though it was not one of my best. 'I was trying to catch a rabbit for your dinner, Colonel.'

'All is not lost, René,' he said reassuringly. 'Lieutenant Gruber has accepted the challenge on your behalf.'

'Lieutenant Gruber is going to fight the undertaker?' I asked.

Unfortunately not. Hubert was to be my second –

never, as he put it, too far behind me. And Edith was selling tickets for the front row and worrying about the catering.

3 MAY

Today Hubert had to present my compliments to Monsieur Alfonse, and agree with him the time and the place. I suggested South America, the Christmas after next.

Edith suggested dawn tomorrow.

Dawn tomorrow it is.

I'm glad to say that the Colonel came up with a plan immediately to improve my chances of survival. He and the Captain will take the troops out on manœuvres tomorrow morning and blow the undertaker away with a twenty-five-pound shell. I should be safe unless the Captain is pulling the trigger.

Not for the first time, I reflect that war makes for some strange bedfellows, as long as you're in the right sort of mood. As I select a sturdy coal-scuttle to use as a breastplate in case of emergency, I feel better now that the German Army is behind me. Just so long as that doesn't include Lieutenant Gruber.

Yvette tells me comfortingly that Monsieur Alfonse is a crack shot, and has put one of his balls through a playing card at twenty-five paces. I'm surprised he doesn't walk with a limp.

The only piece of good news this evening is that the balloon is nearly ready, and the British airmen will soon be leaving. They are getting on my nerves even more than usual. That stupid fool Crabtree has dressed them up as gendarmes and given them a lightning course in what he calls 'the French longwodge'. I have a terrible feeling that if Crabtree is anything to go by they'll start trying to arrest people any minute.

I had another nasty moment later on. Edith interrupted me whilst I was disciplining Maria in the cupboard under the stairs. I explained to her that I was very reluctant to tear a strip off her in front of the customers.

5 MAY

I'll be honest with you. Yesterday was not a lot of fun, even for a hero of the Resistance. Edith disturbed me very early. If you saw her at that time of the morning, I think you'd know what I mean.

'Really René,' she complained when I said I thought I might have a little lie-in. 'You'd be late for your own funeral.'

Lt Gruber does his best to make an old man happy

'Not if that undertaker of yours has anything to do with it,' I quipped bravely.

I rang Monsieur Alfonse at half-past five, just in case he was in the mood to do a deal. I wasn't sure if he was fully acquainted with my reputation for heroism. He said that he was, and that yes, he would come to a special arrangement. He would bury me at trade prices.

So there I was at seven, back to back with the undertaker, a pistol in my hand and a coal scuttle between here and eternity. As I looked around at the crowd that Edith had so thoughtfully gathered, I was impressed by how cleverly the Colonel's troops had hidden themselves. I couldn't spot a single one.

'Before I start counting, René,' Lieutenant Gruber said, 'I have to tell you that the Colonel and the Captain have been arrrested by the Gestapo on suspicion of having sent the Fuhrer an empty knockwurst. Experts have apparently pieced together the wreckage of the Berlin train and found not a trace of The Fallen Madonna, or either of her boobies.'

'What about the manœuvres?' I asked, slightly apprehensively.

'They have, of course, been cancelled. But do not worry, my friend. I am right behind you.'

In that case, I thought, I had no alternative but to run. I owed it to France to live and fight another day. So that is why I am writing these pages in a haystack some distance away from yesterday morning's events. I count myself lucky that I not only wore the coal-scuttle but had you, dear Diary, in my back pocket. In spite of the fact that I was zigzagging through the woods, Monsieur Alfonse still managed to put a dent in me from seventy-five paces. Yvette's warning rang in my mind. Despite his appearance, the undertaker obviously had a lot of balls.

Michelle of the Resistance chose the same haystack for a secret meeting to decide on what course of action to take next. I suggested getting me to Switzerland.

Although I think she understood my reasoning, it is not to be. I am needed too badly at the front.

'You are a vital link in the escape route of the British airmen. Their balloon is assembled and a favourable wind is expected. We will need you to take them to the rendezvous.'

'In these clothes I am a bit conspicuous,' I said. (I am still wearing a top hat and coal-scuttle.)

'Well, take off your clothes.'

'The Resistance don't mess around, do they?' I said. 'But I'm a little old-fashioned about these things. Could we not kiss and cuddle a bit first?'

I must have embarrassed her, because she suddenly pretended she had something else in mind.

'It is so you can put on your disguise,' she said.

I will stop writing and put it on.

6 MAY

I was escorted back to the café by three girls of the Resistance. My disguise was rather daring in the cirumstances: mac, beret, wig, blouse, skirt and short socks. You will appreciate why I'll admit this only once. Monsieur Alfonse, for the time being, was not a worry. Lieutenant Gruber, however, most definitely was.

I don't know why, but he spotted me immediately. 'I'd recognise those legs anywhere, René,' he said, smiling that little smile of his. 'But do not fear. Your secret is safe with me.'

'No, you do not understand,' I said.

'Yes I do, my dear René. I had an uncle with similar leanings. Every Shrove Tuesday, he would dress up as a pancake girl.'

'I suppose you think I am a coward,' I said.

'On the contrary,' he replied. 'I think it takes great courage to come out in the open and dress that way.'

Word had reached me that Herr Flick thought I might have had something to do with the Fuhrer being cheated of the painting of The Fallen Madonna, so when two

Gestapo officers goosestepped into the restaurant I had no choice but to take up Hubert's offer of a dance.

'Keep calm, René,' he said. 'A couple of turns and then I will put you in my little tank and take you back to my place until all this dies down.' He went off to warm it up.

I retreated into the back room to adjust my skirt, to be greeted by a strangely familiar whiff of embalming fluid.

'Monsieur Alfonse,' I said jovially. 'What a pleasant surprise! I expect you are wondering why I decided not to shoot you between the eyes –'

'Nonsense, my dear Artois,' he cried. 'Michelle of the Resistance has explained everything. A bumble-bee down the trousers can unsettle even the bravest man in all France. The leader of the escape route – I had no idea! Let me kiss the hem of your dress!'

Modestly, I looked round for Michelle. She had disappeared like a phantom into the little girl's room, so reluctantly, I took the credit that was due to me.

'Just tell me what to do.' The undertaker embraced me. 'I will follow you anywhere. Vive la France!'

'Vive de Gaulle,' I said.

'Who?'

'De Gaulle. The tall one with the big hooter.'

Now he has left I have nipped down into the cellar to write a page or two. I ...

13 MAY

Helga had burst in.

'Come,' she said. 'The Colonel and Captain are being tortured in Herr Flick's dungeon. We must help them before it is too late.'

'I cannot go like this,' I said. 'I am dressed as a girl.'

'How you relax off-duty is no concern of the German Army. You have not seen the Colonel let his hair down.'

'He hasn't got much,' I replied. 'And he's nearly always wearing a flying helmet.'

It was a short trip to the dungeons of the Gestapo HQ. Engelbert Von Smallhausen, Herr Flick's sidekick, arrested me on the way out of the café. He almost didn't let me bring my handbag.

I will try to draw a veil over the terrible week that followed. The ceiling of the dungeon descended at a signal from Herr Flick, almost crushing us. We had to watch, helpless, as he played with his organ. The Colonel and the Captain took their death pills, which failed to work. My lipstick got smudged.

In the nick of time we were liberated by the very man who had ordered my previous execution. General Von Klinkerhoffen, whose opinion of the Gestapo clearly matches my own, shot the lock off the dungeon door in a fit of rage.

'You cannot do this,' Flick shouted. 'My godfather is Heinrich Himmler.'

Klinkerhoffen was unimpressed. 'My wife's sister is the mistress of Hermann Goering,' he replied. 'The one who wears chamois leather underclothes.'

Fascinated as I was by this exchange, I felt it was time to leave.

'Ladies first,' I said.

War makes for some strange bedfellows

General Von Klinkerhoffen has ordered that the Colonel's manœuvres be resumed.

'The town is ringed with German soldiers. We are under curfew,' Yvette told me breathlessly. I suggested a quiet night in.

Michelle had other ideas. She is always coming to the café with some excuse or other. I have had a terrible feeling since the episode in the haystack that her feelings for me are not simply those of an innocent young girl towards a hero of the Resistance.

This very same afternoon I found myself disguised as an undertaker, smuggling the two British airmen in one of Monsieur Alfonse's hearses. The wind was in the right direction, finally, for England.

The undertaker spoke the words a grateful nation knew would embarrass me: 'I cannot say what an honour it is for me to assist you, Monsieur René – the bravest man in France, who has just escaped death by Gestapo torture and without thought of his personal danger, is even now helping the British airmen to escape.'

'Can I have that in writing?' I asked.

'Only if you write it,' said Edith, inexplicably. 'It is not your plan, it is the plan of Michelle. If you had your way, you would be in bed.'

'Of course,' Monsieur Alfonse said. 'As a lover he is also a legend.'

'You are too kind,' I said.

'Yes he is,' echoed Edith.

General Von Klinkerhoffen himself cut her short by halting the cortège and opening one of the three coffins to check if we were on our way to a real funeral. Fortunately he chose the casket occupied by my widow's mother. One look was enough. White-faced and shaking, he waved us on.

The airmen filled the balloon and floated into the gathering dusk. 'Thanks awfully for having us,' they said, whatever that means. I was almost sad to see them go.

15 MAY

No I wasn't. They're back.

The wind changed direction, and one shot from Von Klinkerhoffen's pistol convinced the idiots to turn off the burner, so they wouldn't be seen in the dark. They crashed through the ceiling of the bedroom of my widow's mother early this morning, just as we were getting her back out of her coffin.

It is now even more draughty in there than usual.

16 MAY

General Von Klinkerhoffen has taken personal command of all troops in the Nouvion district. My heroic Resistance activities have apparently delayed the Fuhrer's victory for many months, and the High Command is worried.

The Colonel isn't too happy either. He has been told by the General that he is short of intelligence, and what's worse, has been ordered to have an affair with Edith to try and improve the situation.

I have to say I didn't immediately see the connection, but Captain Geering tells me that Von Klinkerhoffen believes that amorous liaisons with local girls pay good dividends.

'We have tried this,' the Colonel told him.

'Lots of times,' piped the Captain.

'Did you learn anything new?' asked the General.

'One or two things,' they admitted, but it wasn't enough to get them off the hook.

18 MAY

Hans looked rather glum when he came in for his usual.

'A hard day at the office, Captain?' I asked as I placed a carafe of fine house wine at his disposal.

'I should coco. We have a new intake of privates at the barracks. They are very badly trained. When they are given the order to stand to attention, they stand at ease. When they are told to stand at ease, they fall out. It is a shambles.'

'Trouble?' asked Lieutenant Gruber, pulling up a chair.

'It is the Colonel,' I said. 'He is having a bit of trouble with his privates.'

'Oh?'

'Yes, they keep falling out.'

'Has he tried a change of clothing?'

'Yes,' said Hans, 'but that did no good. Now General Von Klinkerhoffen has told him to clap them in irons. The Colonel is very worried.'

'I imagine he would be. I have a designer friend in Berlin from my window-dressing days I could refer him to . . .'

23 MAY

It's been a quiet week for business, so I decided this morning to put in a bit of time on the billiard table with Yvette. When I arrived in the games room I was slightly surprised to discover that she had already started.

'I was just practising, René,' she said. 'Look at this position. I am right up against the cushion and have no alternative but to screw the length of the table.'

Not for the first time I realised there was very little I could teach Yvette.

We had hardly started the session when Edith and Michelle arrived. My fellow heroes of the Resistance had decided that they could not operate under the cruel

tyranny of General Von Klinkerhoffen. He had to be killed.

Edith had a plan. 'René, you could deliver him some food and round your waist you could strap dynamite, and when you got near him you could light the fuse and – whoof – he would be gone and you would be buried as a great hero of the Resistance.'

I had a plan too. It involved checking the effectiveness of the escape route to Switzerland.

Herr Flick and Helga also have a plan. I had my ear to the keyhole of the back room whilst they were entertaining each other last night. I often do this. It is my way of monitoring the enjoyment of my customers without imposing myself upon them.

On this occasion, however, they were not complimenting the cuisine. They were organising the assassination of Von Klinkerhoffen with a poisoned dart shot from a blow-pipe.

'He's about to be rubbed out,' I told Maria. 'Poof! With a cigarette holder.'

She glanced across at Lieutenant Gruber, who was tickling the ivories in the corner of the restaurant. 'And he plays the piano so beautifully,' she said sadly.

I was about to put her right when the Colonel came in. He has not been to the café since Von Klinkerhoffen ordered him to have an affair with my wife. He has finally found a solution to the problem. Or rather, two solutions.

The first was for the Captain to have the affair.

'There is not another singer like you in the whole world,' he piped when Edith had finished a number. She rewarded his gallantry with a kiss that steamed up his glasses. 'Oh Captain,' she breathed when he removed them for wiping, 'without glasses you are even more attractive.'

'So are you!' he said.

The second was to kill the General, who was clearly less popular than I had assumed. The Captain would poison him with a drug in a jug of wine at the forthcoming party at the château to celebrate the Kaiser's birthday.

Life is getting complicated again.

The two British airmen have found a way of phoning Wimbledon on the radio transmitter, and I'm very worried about the bill. And Edith is to bake a gâteau for the château which is to be filled with dynamite. The fuse will be a candle with a handle. I would have thought the cake alone should do the trick.

This party is going to make the burning of the Reichstag look like an evening with my wife's mother. I have a terrible feeling it is not going to be good for business.

Carstairs and Fairfax trying to remember the number of the Wimbledon exchange

26 MAY

Now I know it is not going to be good for business. Herr Flick of the Gestapo has given instructions for the party to be held at the café instead. And everybody is invited for tomorrow night.

A Song for the Boys in the Tank Corps
(Especially "B" Troop)

If you ever get across the sea to England,
Then maybe at the closing of the day,
The bars will all be serving German lager,
Which means we've won the war
Hip hip hooray."...

27 MAY

I could not live with the possibility that innocent heroes of the Resistance might be killed, and in my restaurant. I had to take action.

Von Klinkerhoffen borrowed Helga's cigarette holder before she could use it on him, so Herr Flick took the dart on the nose instead. But then I had to deal with the drug in the jug and the candle with the handle on the gâteau for the château.

After swopping the Captain's poison pill with an aspirin, things were still desperate. The General lit the candle with the handle and the fire bucket was the only answer.

I'm not sure he was overjoyed when I covered the gateau with a pile of sand. 'You fool,' he screamed. 'We were celebrating the moment of the Kaiser's birth!'

'I meant no disrespect, General,' I said cleverly. 'I am celebrating the moment of his heroic burial.'

31 MAY

This war is starting to take its toll. It is three days since *Le Café René* narrowly avoided becoming a five-star hole in the ground, and my nerves still need considerable soothing. I was luxuriating in a warm bath this morning and Yvette, ever solicitous, asked if I was ready for two big jugs. I was.

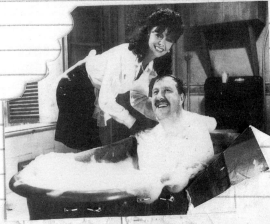

Yvette lets René
have it with both jugs

'Sorry it took so long, René,' she said. 'The old boiler is in a terrible state.'

'I don't know why I married her in the first place,' I replied.

I had scarcely begun to enjoy the second jug when there was a knock on the window. It was Michelle.

'I shall say this only once,' she said, 'because I am clinging to a rusty drainpipe. I have a plan to get rid of the British airmen –'

Unluckily for her the drainpipe gave way before she could go any further.

Later on I found myself telling Lieutenant Gruber about the difficulties of finding sufficient privacy to attend to one's toilet. He was very understanding.

'I have a very large bath at the château if you ever want to indulge yourslf, René.'

I suddenly decided to change the subject. 'Excuse me, Lieutenant,' I said. 'I can't help noticing that my wife has just finished one of her songs. Some of my other customers may need help.'

'She has an unusual voice,' he said, unwilling to lose me. 'Was it trained?'

'It was,' I replied. 'But it escaped and returned to the wild.'

1 JUNE

Michelle of the Resistance did not have a happy landing yesterday. She appeared last night with her leg in plaster, supported by that fool Crabtree who thinks he can speak our language. Her plan is to steal a plane with no engine from the Nouvion Transport Museum, fix it up with the engine from General Von Klinkerhoffen's motor mower, and bingo, no airmen.

I wondered whether she had taken a sharp blow to the head as well. 'Who will steal this plane?' I asked, knowing that she would find it hard to entrust a task like this to anyone else.

I was right.

'You will,' she whispered only once.

2 JUNE

I had my ear to the keyhole of the back room at lunchtime, anxious to know Herr Flick's opinion of the *Culotte de Bœuf René aux Flageolets* when I overheard a conversation of a rather different kind.

'I have bad news,' Von Smallhausen reported. 'The Resistance have kidnapped your knockwurst and are demanding a ransom for its return. I received this information at ten o'clock this morning.'

'That was four hours ago,' Flick said coldly. 'Why did you take so long to inform me?'

'This message was wrapped round a brick and thrown at my head. I have only just regained consciousness.'

'It is very serious. Helga, your Colonel is in charge of security. Tell him that if the knockwurst is not recovered he is to burn down Nouvion – except for this building.'

I had a sudden image of *Le Café René* standing in the midst of the ashes, the only café for miles around. It was dreadful news, but I resolved to make the best of it.

3 JUNE

It is the Communist Resistance causing all the trouble, as usual. They want eight thousand francs before they return what Herr Flick thinks is the real painting of The Fallen Madonna with the Big Boobies by Van Clomp. If the money is not found, the sausage will be sliced. If the sausage is sliced, the town will burn.

Edith tells me that Monsieur Alfonse has eight thousand francs hidden in his mattress. How she found this out, I can only guess.

She is at this very moment attempting to persuade the old man to lend it to us so that we can give it to the Communists in return for the painting and then ambush them and get it back.

I'd rather not speculate on how she intends to do it, but I know that for some reason my wife makes him feel like a man twenty years younger. I should think he does the same for her.

4 JUNE

Things didn't quite go according to plan.

Edith got the money from Monsieur Alfonse. The Communist Resistance got the money from us. Unfortunately one of Lieutenant Gruber's very large dogs got the knockwurst, and because the ambush was a complete failure we will never see the eight thousand francs again either.

In future I must take responsibility for everything myself. I should know by now that whilst it is all very well having people under me, I should never let them take the lead.

5 JUNE

How do you tell an old undertaker with a weak heart that his entire life savings have gone? By phone, I suppose.

I'm not a man to delay things, but I might leave it until next week.

12 JUNE

It has not been an easy week for Lieutenant Gruber either. As he was taking his little tank out for a spin this afternoon he dropped by the café to tell me about it.

'Herr Flick is not pleased that my dog, Eric, stole his sausage. "Gruber," he said, "have you been mincing?"'

'Well, had you?'

'Of course. Eric only likes his knockwurst chopped up very finely.'

'What about the painting?'

'He wasn't too happy about that either, until I told him that actually it was a forgery.'

Somehow I don't think we've heard the last of The Fallen Madonna with the Big Boobies.

13 JUNE

I was right.

Herr Flick is under the impression that there is a certain hero of the Resistance not a million miles away from here who had something to do with his Van Clomp being switched with a forgery. He has ordered Lieutenant Gruber to drive his little tank from where it is parked outside the front of the café into the garden at the back. In a straight line.

I had to think fast. I realised that I would have to tell Hubert the truth about the paintings.

'How would it be if we substituted another forgery in another sausage?' he suggested. 'I think I could provide a copy if I could see the original.'

'I didn't know you were an artist,' I said.

'I have leanings, you know,' he replied, 'and not a little talent. Before I was a window dresser I was employed in an art gallery. Occasionally I was allowed to touch up old masters.'

With that, he asked if we could go down to the cellar to look at my masterpiece. I can see this is going to be very complicated.

23 JUNE

I haven't had time for writing much recently. The mid-year accounts have been occupying most of my waking thoughts.

Yvette's and Maria's figures have been holding up well, and in some areas have even shown signs of improvement. Losses in other parts of the business, however, have been appalling. This has partly to do with the fact that Edith has been spending most of the bar takings on hats. The rest I blame on Monsieur Alfonse. I paid him back eight thousand francs forged by the idiot Leclerc, and he promptly went and spent them in the café as a tribute to my heroism.

24 JUNE

Lieutenant Gruber was very anxious that I bring the real painting of The Fallen Madonna to his room in the château so he could start on the copy. I had a shrewd suspicion I might get invited to stay on and see his etchings.

Unfortunately I was far too busy today to go myself, and sent Maria instead, with the canvas concealed about her bosom. She has been captured by General Von Klinkerhoffen, who did not believe that she had an appointment with Lieutenant Gruber even when she showed him the knockwurst.

So now both Maria and the knockwurst, which is a whopper, are imprisoned in the General's wardrobe, and he is demanding the return of the engine of his motor mower in return for their freedom. And without the engine we won't be able to rid ourselves of the two British airmen.

It will take a genius to get them out.

25 JUNE

I spent a lot of last night hiding under General Von Klinkerhoffen's bed with Yvette. It was touch and go, I must say, and at one stage, as I explained to Edith when she found us there, I had to revive the young girl with the heat of my body. She had fainted with excitement.

Suffice it to say that my daring undercover work paid off, and both Maria and the knockwurst are now safely back in the cellar of the café. I must go down and see if she is any the worse for her ordeal.

26 JUNE

Michelle of the Resistance is still wedded to this hare-brained scheme to steal the aeroplane without the engine. There is one big problem, however: it is at the very back of the Transport Museum, with many antique vehicles in the way. She has spent most of the time since her accident trying to think of a way round.

I told her that I'd be prepared to forget the whole thing. I'm pretty sure that General de Gaulle, the one with the big hooter, will be calling on the transmitter any minute to award me a whole string of medals – so what's one more?

*Yvette dusts up her technique
in the General's bedroom*

27 JUNE

She has found a way. The Germans have given permission for us to hold an Antique Vehicle Rally tomorrow. The plan is to move everything out of the way of the plane, insert the engine from the mower, then attach it to a car with a very long piece of elastic. The car will be driven from the museum at great speed by a hero of the Resistance, thereby catapulting the two British airmen back across the Channel.

There was a call from London this morning. I thought it was de Gaulle, but he is obviously still busy thinking about my medals. In fact it was the C.O. of the two airmen, Wing Commander Randy Hargreaves. He is desperate for them to return immediately. The war must be going very badly for them.

A message also arrived from Lieutenant Gruber. He wanted to get his hands on The Fallen Madonna. This was a bit of a turn up.

I invited him into the back room. 'A rare honour, René,' he beamed as he came in. 'It is the first time I have seen your rear quarters. This is very cosy.'

Before he got any cosier, I suggested we go upstairs and find the knockwurst containing the painting, which I had hidden in my bed. This seemed very popular with the Lieutenant.

I was horrified to see that Edith had got there first. Even worse, she was in the process of giving the knockwurst a little nibble.*

'What are you doing with that sausage?' I cried.

'I prayed to God and he left it under my bed.'

'You prayed to God for a sausage?' This was a new one on me.

'No,' she replied, 'but this was obviously as near as He could get.'

'Rationing,' I said to Lieutenant Gruber on the way down, 'can be very frustrating.'

30 JUNE

It is not usual for a hero of the Resistance to complain, but my body has taken a lot of punishment in the last few days. In fact I am being tended to by Yvette as I write, so forgive me if my hand starts to wander.

We collected enough braces from the patriots of Nouvion to make the catapult for the plane. They had been dropping them in the bar for the last twenty-four hours, and Lieutenant Gruber couldn't believe his luck.

I bared my torso for France on the afternoon of the Antique Vehicle Rally, disguised as a road mender. There

---

* *I know how easy this can be.*

was only one nasty moment when the Lieutenant appeared in his little tank and pointed his big gun at me.

Soon Michelle signalled that all the obstacles had been cleared and the plane was ready for take-off. I got into the car and moved it skilfully through the gears. I was soon travelling at an incredible speed, with the elastic stretching out behind me. As I turned to wave at Yvette and Maria, the earth moved.

I thought at first that Edith, who was in the passenger seat, had given me a sharp blow to the head. In fact the chocks had jammed in front of the aircraft's wheels and a very unhappy hero of the Resistance was catapulted back into the Transport Museum.

I don't know where my wife landed, but there was some suggestion afterwards that she be placed on permanent display as an intercontinental ballistic missile.

30 JULY

There cannot be many French café-owners languishing in a prisoner-of-war camp in the borrowed uniform of a British Flight Lieutenant, and it is a little unusual even for a hero of the Resistance.

How did I get here? It's a long story, but since paper is so scarce in this place I will cut it very short. I'll only go back about seventy years or so to when my wife's mother was having it off in Avignon with a weirdo from Holland she called Bobby. Bobby was a painter, but a very unsuccessful one. The story goes that the poor fellow was so hungry he once even ate one of his own ears. My own theory is that it was a last-ditch attempt to escape the nagging of my wife's mother. Anyway his paintings were awful. Not very lifelike at all. He seemed to specialise in close-ups of sunflowers and wobbly old chairs. That's the impression I get, anyway.

Now, one of his terrible efforts was called the Cracked Vase with the Big Daisies. He gave it to my wife's mother as a memento one day just before he went out into the

sunflower field and blew his head off. Looking at early pictures of my wife's mother, I can understand his desperation.

Anyway, this is the painting which hangs in the café, and behind which yesterday I hid the painting of The Fallen Madonna with the Big Boobies by Van Clomp when all the world and his wife seemed to be hunting for it. General Von Klinkerhoffen, too, was on the hunt – for the two British airmen. But he didn't find them. They were hiding in the café, disguised as French tarts. They melted easily into the crowd.

The General did spot, however, the painting of the Cracked Vase with the Big Daisies, and he requisitioned it. He thinks it was done by someone called Vincent Van Gogh and has commmissioned Lieutenant Gruber to make a copy of it. Good luck to him, I say. There's no acounting for taste.

Meanwhile, Monsieur Alfonse was busy tunnelling from his mortuary towards the prisoner-of-war camp so that the two airmen could be smuggled into it for safe keeping. The tunnelling was not progressing fast enough for my liking, however. I got my tool out and asked Yvette what she thought of it. She seemed impressed, and asked me if she could have a go with it. I always knew that little pick would come in handy one day.

Unfortunately, the Colonel and the Captain discovered the tunnel while Edith, Yvette, Maria and I were all down it. The tunnel collapsed behind them, and we had no alternative but to surface in the camp.

Now how can I get out of here? Your guess is as good as mine. In my experience British Flight Lieutenants don't have a very good record for getting out of anywhere.

31 JULY

I spent most of today holding my trousers open at the top while Yvette and Edith filled them up with soil.

You will find this hard to believe, but the German guards (or 'goons' as we British Flight Lieutenants prefer to call them) then found nothing suspicious about the hang of my trousers as I waddled out of the hut nearly a hundred times like the Michelin man with haemorrhoids, undid my cycle clips, and then walked all around the vegetable patch while shaking my legs vigorously. If they don't find that sort of behaviour just a little bit worth looking into then I reckon they deserve to lose the war. Or maybe it's just that they understand the ways of the British better than I.

Ah me, will there ever be an end to the madness of war, I ask myself? Will there ever be an end to the unrelenting hardship and danger of digging this tunnel? And more to the point, will there ever be an end to the merciless chafing of my soiled underwear?

Whatever happens, I must get out of here soon. The café opens at six o'clock and I have a business to run. And *merde!* I am now down to writing on toilet paper.

1 AUGUST

Another day, another hundred trouser-loads of earth.

Edith was beginning to get decidedly edgy. 'I hope I am not expected to sleep in this hut with forty desperate men,' she said.

'They are only desperate to get out, Edith,' I muttered.

But there was no need for her to get her hideous French knickers in a twist. While shaking out his trousers in the vegetable patch a humble Normandy café-owner had had a blinding flash, and even as his wife spoke he was sketching it out in his diary for the British escape committee.

2 AUGUST

Tonight I am to be a Bluebell Girl in the Camp Concert – and with a title like that to the show, I can't help feeling how lucky it is that Lieutenant Gruber is otherwise engaged.

It has been quite a busy day, rehearsing my high kick routine and timing my splits to perfection. Luckily carrying around all that earth from the tunnel has done marvellous things for my legs. I will certainly be able to be much more energetic next time Yvette needs my help in the cellar.

The Colonel and the Captain took to the cricket field

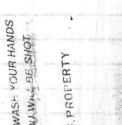

this afternoon, but by all accounts the cricket field did not take to them. The game ended when the Commandant's window got broken, and the Commandant got very cross. Shortly afterwards, Captain Hans went for the big one over square leg with the help of the plank across the barrel and yours truly off the hut roof with half a ton of soil in his trousers. He should be on his way now to fetch Lieutenant Gruber's little tank so that he can smash down the wire and rescue us.

Oh, what a lovely war!

Well that's show business for you. One moment you are a star and the next you are on the rubbish heap. Lieutenant Gruber has rescued us by disguising himself as a dustcart driver and taking us away amongst the tea-leaves and old

fish-heads. Heaven only knows what Fate holds in store for us now. I suppose I could always read the tea-leaves to find out.

It appears that the brilliant rescue plan was both his and Helga's. They took the view that we are in this together: we all share an interest, after all, in certain paintings which we will sell after the war. Besides, Gruber felt the café was just not the same without me.

To get the message to us about their plan, one of them had appeared at the camp gate dressed like Marlene Dietrich, in a brimmed hat and raincoat which opened to reveal lascivious underwear and a lot of leg. Much to my surprise, it was not Gruber. *He* was dressed as a nun.

Well, everything went according to plan – except for one little thing. The two British airmen who were supposed to stay behind in the camp followed us into the dustcart and have escaped as well. So now we're right back to square one. What's more, the Colonel is now sitting in my cellar, dressed as a girl from the Folies Bergères.

He cannot leave, even in borrowed clothes, because of the curfew. And we've also heard that the Captain has been taken away by the Communist Resistance. Michelle thought they were on strike, but apparently they've settled for higher ransoms.

Maria did not escape with us. Michelle has just brought news of her. She broke into the postal room of the prisoner-of-war camp and disguised herself as a Red Cross parcel. Unfortunately she did not put on enough stamps so she has been sent back to Switzerland. So now we must advertise for a new girl. Is there no end to it?

4 AUGUST

No, there isn't. We also nearly got nicked last night by Herr Flick. He, along with that overgrown fruit-bat, Von Smallhausen, had climbed onto the roof of Gestapo headquarters and jammed the broadcast from London, substituting a message of their own.

Of course, we weren't to know that. ''Allo Nighthawk, we wish to send medals to the members of the Resistance,' came the totally innocent request. 'Please give me their names and addresses.'

I had to give the honest answer. 'We do not know their names and addresses, but send me the medals and I will pass them on.'

It was then that they made the sort of mistake that a highly alert Resistance brain was able to detect at once. In the backgound I heard a strange sliding noise and Von Smallhausen's suddenly receding voice. 'Herr Flick,' he observed as he plummeted into space, 'I am falling off the roof ...'

In the heat of the moment and for the good of France, I threw the radio out of the window. It is my wife that we must then thank for coming up with idea of using the radio in Lieutenant Gruber's little tank to continue our conversation with London. To create a diversion, I got the

Lieutenant to sing me a song at the piano. His choice was *Mad About The Boy*. Well it would be, wouldn't it? He fixed his eyes on me as he sang. It wasn't going to be easy to get away.

'Lieutenant Gruber, your singing is so beautiful I will have to go outside. I do not like crying in front of men.'

'I understand,' he said. 'I feel quite emotional myself.'

On that note, I went to join the others in Lieutenant Gruber's little tank. Unfortunately, the idiot policeman who thinks he can speak our language overheard the noise of the radio and reported us to the Colonel. He caught us red-handed.

'René,' he said rather crossly, 'what are you doing in Gruber's little tank?'

'Well, Colonel, we heard the telephone ringing so we just popped in to answer it. Just in case it was anyone important for you – you know, like Hitler.'

That was definitely enough quick thinking for one humble café-owner for one day. I was ready for a bit of a lie-down. I was just looking around for Yvette when Gruber's receiver crackled and London came through again.* Who of all people should be on the other end but Captain Geering? He was in an office overlooking Piccadilly Circus. He sounded surprisingly happy. He said he wasn't coming back.

'What am I going to tell the General?' the Colonel asked.

'Tell him the food is very good and the British think they are going to win. Over and out.'

20 AUGUST

If you could see me now, dear Diary, you would be asking yourself why it is that I am wearing a clean new apron today, and why it is that I have trimmed my moustache and manicured my nails. If you were standing next to me you would know that I am also wearing a very powerful after-shave lotion. My wife finds it irresistible so I seldom wear it, but this is a special occasion. I have advertised for a girl to work under me in the bar and there have been many applicants. Today is interview day. Unfortunately, rather too many interested parties for my liking have opted themselves onto the selection committee ...

---

* *How typical of the altruism of René Artois that he should worry about the whereabouts of his staff in a moment of crisis. It is only to be hoped that he managed to find my mother and so relieve his tension.*

APPLICANT: Madame Sablon
SPECIAL ABILITIES: Elderly. Walks with a stick.
EDITH'S COMMENTS: Very suitable.
MY COMMENTS: Rejected solely on the grounds that she wouldn't be able to get on her knees to scrub the floor, or climb the stairs to entertain the Germans.

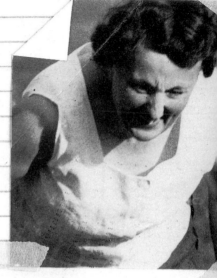

APPLICANT: Mademoiselle Angelique Vitesse
SPECIAL ABILITIES: 38–28–38
EDITH'S COMMENTS: Next please.
MY COMMENTS: Youthful and enthusiastic. Would have worked well under me.

APPLICANT: Mademoiselle Valérie Vendôme
SPECIAL ABILITIES: Until recently worked in a circus.
Can ride one-wheel bicycle and perform cartwheels crabs
and other acrobatics. Also sings
beautifully and does cabaret.
EDITH'S COMMENTS: So do I.
Next please.
MY COMMENTS: Her skills
might have come in handy for
errands and dusting under the beds.

APPLICANT: Mimi Labonq
SPECIAL ABILITIES: Resistance gang leader in Paris.
Martial arts expert. Can knock café-owners to the floor
with one blow.
EDITH'S COMMENTS: Good
– she is hired.
MY COMMENTS: Michelle of
the Resistance is pointing
a gun at me.

21 AUGUST

A day of shocks, starting when Herr Flick of the Gestapo arrived with Helga in his staff car. Helga was driving.

'You drive well,' I overheard him say to her as I collected cups from the tables outside my humble café.

'Thank you, Herr Flick,' Helga replied. 'I am, however, not good at reversing.'

'You managed very well last night.'

I only just recovered in time to greet them at the door.

'Welcome to my humble café, Herr Flick,' I said. 'Let me take from you your sinister leather coat.' I led them to their usual table in the back room – only to find Crabtree behind the curtains.

'Good evening, officer,' I said. 'How comforting to know that you are doing your duty.'

'It is a dick night. I thought I saw two men leaking by your dustbins.'

'Well,' I said, 'that's France for you.'

More shocks were to follow. With my ear to the keyhole of the private dining room, I overheard the following conversation:

'Herr Flick, when you behave in such a dominating fashion I go weak at the knees.'

'Only the knees?'

'I am blushing.'

'This is normal. Helga, I wish you to know that this is a very special occasion. I have decided to marry you.'

'Herr Flick, I thought we were going to wait until after the war?'

'These are dangerous times, Helga. We must grab every moment of happiness while we can.'

'But Herr Flick, you have managed to grab it so far without getting married.'

Herr Flick drives Helga to the country . . .

. . . and shows her his knob

24 AUGUST

I met the Colonel's new assistant tonight – Captain Alberto Bertorelli. He is an Itie. An Italian unit will be going with the Germans when they invade England. Well, I suppose somebody has to take over the ice-cream business.

Bertorelli wears a lot of medals. Some for service in Abyssinia. Some for service in North Africa. Some, I suspect, simply for servicing Fiats.

When he entered the café he kissed me.

'I am just a humble peasant you understand,' I told him. 'Trying to scratch a living with my wife's mother and my wife.'

'I embrace your wife,' he said, embracing Yvette.

'I embrace your mother-in-law,' he said, embracing Edith.

Close to tears, Edith stormed from the room. I might give Bertorelli a medal of my own.

I put my ear to the keyhole tonight as Herr Flick and Helga were finishing their meal. I always like to check how my diners are getting on with each other – whether it's another bottle of champagne they'll be needing, or just two coffees.

'I have been giving much thought to the arrangements for our wedding,' I overheard Herr Flick say.

'Herr Flick,' said Helga's gentle Aryan voice, 'are you sure that deep in your heart, wherever it is, you are ready for marriage?'

'What are you saying?'

'Well, you are so young, so attractive – women are always throwing themselves at you.'

'This is true.'

'I will be consumed with jealousy. I will be breaking plates when I do the washing-up.'

'If you do that you will be punished. We will be married in a high security Gestapo chapel. As we leave the ceremony we will walk through an arch of rubber truncheons held by my Gestapo colleagues in jackboots. We will drive away in a black Gestapo limousine showered with propaganda pamphlets. We will honeymoon in a Bavarian forest. Every morning we will leave our camouflaged tent, strip naked and dive into the icy waters of a limpid dark lake.'

'Could I have time to think about it?'

Ah, just the two coffees, then.

1 SEPTEMBER

Things are looking up. A slip of the tongue by the Colonel has revealed to me that the Germans are soon to invade England. Churchill will, of course, throw in the sponge. The war will be over in a few weeks and life will return to normal at *Le Café René*.

Things are looking down.

Michelle of the Resistance came round to tell me that I need more length. The Gestapo are jamming our broadcasts to London, and to give us a stronger signal she has arranged for a kite to be constructed which will take my aerial to the required height. Mimi is in charge of collecting

Michelle tells René he needs more length

this kite from the convent. To avoid suspicion she is to be disguised as a small nun. Well, she could hardly be disguised as a big one, could she?

'Cannot you do some of this?' I asked. Little did I know that things have obviously been getting on top of her.

'Why is it that you always question my decisions?' she snapped. 'Do you think you could do my job better? Do you think you could run the Resistance keeping everyone happy? Deciding who to shoot, what to blow up, making threatening calls? Do you know what my telephone bill is every month? Why do you not go and work for the Communist Resistance and get up their noses?'

Some people find it hard to take a subordinate role.

'Now look what you have done,' said Edith. 'You have

"All-a night I dream-a of your face,
As I sleep-a in my room;
I tink I must-a be in love,
My heart go boom-titty-
boom-titty-boom."
Alberto Bertorelli
(Captain)

A poem to Madam Edith, a beautiful lady

upset the Resistance.'

Luckily there was a knock at the window at that moment and Crabtree the gendarme appeared.

'Good moaning. Outside your coffee was this bunch of diffadoles and doses. Pinned to them is a nit.'

The nit was from the Italian Captain. It was a terrible poem for Edith.

'He's not the first Itie to have the hots for me,' she said glowingly.

Hah! Just because ten years ago an ice-cream man gave her a free cornet.

4 SEPTEMBER

I led Edith, Mimi and Yvette at lunchtime on an expedition to launch the kite. Edith was carrying a fully loaded picnic basket. Yvette was carrying another picnic basket containing thirty kilograms of batteries. Mimi was bent under the weight of the cripplingly heavy radio pack. I would gladly have helped them but as I explained, I have a lot of trouble with my back.

'Also you have a lot of trouble with your front,' said Edith, rather unnecessarily.

We did not know it at the time, but, as Lieutenant Gruber told me later, General Von Klinkerhoffen and the other German officers were also nearby, inspecting the area where the invasion troops would be assembling.

'That area will be occupied by one regiment of artillery,' said the General. 'In a few months' time there will be two thousand men camping there.'

'Make a note of that, Lieutenant,' said the Colonel.

'I already have,' said Gruber.

Yvette connected the wire to the kite and Edith and Mimi concealed themselves in the bushes with the radio. The moment had at last arrived for me to expose my

'Baroness Von Trapp not ruled out as suspect' say Germans

leadership qualities to the full, to show these girls how willing I was to get it up for France.

Mimi handed me the large coil of wire that had been hanging on the backpack. The other end was attached to the radio. Yvette launched the kite and I ran into the wind as fast as I could. Everything went well until the kite suddenly got caught in a strong gust. The wire began to slip through my hands. It was burning my fingers. Suddenly I could hold it no longer. The rest of the coil started to unwind. When it reached the end Mimi was yanked up out of the bushes and into the sky.

'My God!' Edith screamed. 'We have lost our new waitress.'

'And good staff are so difficult to find,' I said.

Michelle of the Resistance has very kindly brought round a tandem to help me generate more volts. It will go in the bedroom of my wife's mother, because we lost the batteries for the radio crossing the river while rescuing Mimi the flying nun. The dynamo will provide a temporary source of power.

'Will not the Germans be suspicious if they search and find a bicycle in the bedroom of my wife's mother?' I asked.

'You could say that it is a keep-fit machine.'

'Is it not a bit late? She is eighty-six.'

But it will not be for long. Already the Resistance have stolen more batteries from a German midget submarine, it seems. They will be delivered to me by one of her agents.

'Disguised as a torpedo I suppose?' I said.

But the good news does not stop there. More explosives have arrived from London to be used to blow up the safe in the château which contains the plans for the invasion. I will have the honour of storing them in my cellar.

Really, I told her, I appreciate the fact that I am waging a one-man war, but is it too much to ask that she lift just a few of the more minor responsibilities from my shoulders occasionally?

Michelle offered to have the explosives delivered C.O.D. to save me queueing up at the post office. Another of her agents will bring them to me concealed in a secret pouch in his trousers.

'How will I know this man?' I enquired.

'He will be walking very gingerly,' she said.

Lieutenant Gruber came into the café this afternoon looking as if he'd just had a bit of a rough ride in his little tank.

'You may notice that I am walking very gingerly,' he said.

'Do not tell me that you have dynamite in your trousers?' I asked.

'René!' he admonished, 'do not listen to gossip!'

Herr Flick of the Gestapo also came in. At least I thought it was Herr Flick, but it turned out to be Helga, wearing his sinister leather coat and limping. She was wearing Herr Flick's clothes because he has taken hers. She brought serious news which could affect each one of us.

'Herr Flick has disguised himself as a temporary lady stenographer of the female sex. He has concealed a listening device in a daffodil in a vase of flowers on the desk of Colonel Von Strohm.'

'Apart from the satisfaction he obtains from dressing in girls' clothes,' asked Lieutenant Gruber, 'why would he do this?'

It appears that Herr Flick suspects General Von Klinkerhoffen and the Colonel of being involved in a plot to blow up Hitler. If it is true and the Colonel is tortured we will all be implicated because he may reveal that Lieutenant Gruber is painting a forgery of The Fallen Madonna with the Big Boobies and the Van Gogh with the Big Daisies.

Our only hope is that Lieutenant Gruber can warn the Colonel, who has been busily engaged today acquiring novelties for the party to celebrate Goering's birthday.

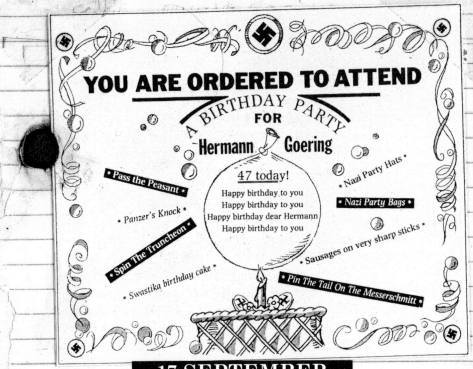

Good news from Lieutenant Gruber. He managed to warn the General about Herr Flick, and 'Irma Von Kinkenrotten' has been arrested and thrown into a dungeon in the château.

Bad news from Michelle of the Resistance. A radio message was due tonight from London, which meant that two volunteers had a lot of pedalling to do on the tandem in the bedroom of my wife's mother. Yvette stepped forward at once and offered her services. She was wearing a silk athletics singlet that was two sizes too small, and very flimsy shorts. I jumped into the saddle behind her at once, eager to let my thighs do their bit for France.

'Your breath is very hot,' she said to me as I pedalled like a mad hamster.

'Your shorts are very thin,' I replied.

19 SEPTEMBER

Fairly quiet day, today. Got up. Got dressed. Got arrested. It seems the Colonel is very cross about the batteries stolen from the German midget submarine.

Edith launched an attempt to rescue me, disguised as a German soldier, but as she left the café, the Itie Bertorelli turned up and Edith had to dive into the pissoir to avoid him. The Itie also went into the pissoir. It was when he left that I, having masterfully negotiated my release with the Colonel so that I could live to fight another day for the glory of France, arrived.

As you can imagine, Edith was overjoyed to be reunited with the bravest man in all France. She presented me with the hand grenade she had been intending to use in her rescue bid. But not before she had taken the pin as a souvenir. I looked at it. I looked at Edith. We looked at each other. We got out of there faster than the British off the beaches of Dunkirk. Seconds later, the convenience blew sky-high. This is going to cause quite a stink, I can tell you.

Anyway, there is rather a pungent postscript to all this business. As I went back to check for survivors and to prevent looting, I discovered amongst the wreckage several envelopes addressed to England. Sadly, the letters

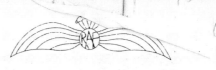

Dear Mummy

I say, Mumsy, Fairfax is a bit down in the old mouth just now.

We got a right old wigging from Smelly Gibson on the Froggies' radio. Seems if we don't escape soon the war will be over. Smelly says we're doing rather badly against the Jerries and it's all costing an awful lot so he's stopped our pay. I say, that's a bit of a rum do, don't you think?

Then Smelly gave Fairfax more bad news. "Your fiancé is getting married on Thursday," he said.

"Deirdre? I can't be back by then," said Fairfax.

"She's marrying Randy Hargreaves. Any message?"

"Yes. Tell her to get stuffed."

"It's a bit late for that."

Oh well, Mumsy, I'll write again soon. Hope this finds you as it leaves me,

Over and out,

Your loving son,

Carstairs

P.S. Any chance of bunging over the odd franc now they've stopped all my tuck money?

P.P.S. Still no news from you. Are you sure you've got the address right?

are all in English so I don't understand a word of them. What they were doing there is a total mystery to me.*

---

* This entry clears the air on an issue that English war historians have been straining over ever since the publication in 1946 of the wartime reminiscences of Monsieur Alfonse, The Wooden Hearse. The mystery was over the non-arrival in England of all the letters which the two British airmen had faithfully posted home to their mothers every Sunday evening. Alfonse wrote of Carstairs' bemusement that 'here in Froggie land the chaps don't seem averse to the odd tinkle in a pillar-box'. Now at last it is clear. They thought the pissoir was for posting letters in.

6 OCTOBER

Helga was very pleased with herself today. Herr Flick, now out of the clink, feels that she has shown great devotion by helping him to perfect his interrogation techniques and has presented her with the Gestapo Certificate of Merit. It is not only a great honour, but with it she can get into the cinema free before five o'clock.

8 OCTOBER

Yvette and Mimi have hatched a plot to steal some film for Michelle's spy camera. Yvette has invited the Colonel to take photographs of her in her underwear, and Mimi will steal the film from the Colonel's camera while Yvette is distracting him with the flying helmet and wet celery. What I wouldn't give to be there myself.*

Michelle has disguised the spy camera as a large potato. Next time they order food from the château I am to deliver it. Then I must get into the room containing the safe and take a photograph so that Monsieur Leclerc, the ex-jailbird, can work out how we can break into it and steal the invasion plans. I will then deliver the film to Monsieur Alfonse, who has, in his mortuary, many fluids which skilfully blended can develop the film.

I tell you, I wish I had stayed with the girls in the typing pool.

---

* *Can one ever cease to marvel at the bravery of this man? No sooner has René escaped from one close shave than he is willing to risk his life all over again in yet another dangerous situation.*

Today General Von Klinkerhoffen decided to let his hair down. He ordered Lieutenant Gruber to arrange a date for him with Helga this evening at the café. Which might have been all right had Herr Flick of the Gestapo not arrived just before the General ...

Everyone in the café fell silent as Flick limped in.

'There is no reason to cease your jollification just because a senior Gestapo officer in a particularly foul mood is entering your premises,' he said. Then he spotted Helga.

'So – there you are. What kind of funny old game is this? I have two tickets for a film featuring Herr Stanley Laurel and Herr Oliver Hardy and I am left waiting in the foyer holding a bag of chocolate fudge ...'

'I am sorry, Herr Flick. I have been ordered by General Von Klinkerhoffen to be his companion for the evening.'

'You will learn, Helga, that nobody stands up the Gestapo.'

'Oh Herr Flick – to see you consumed with jealousy is most stimulating.'

'I am not consumed with jealousy. I am just mad as a snake. You will leave with me now.'

'I cannot. I am obeying orders.'

'I thought that you and I had something good going ...'

To cut a long story short, Herr Flick has arrested Helga and taken her away for lengthy questioning. And Yvette has been taken away by the Colonel with a lengthy bit of celery.

12 OCTOBER

Mission accomplished. I have risked life and limb in the château and a lot more in Gruber's bedroom – but I have the photograph of the safe.

We set off last night as planned. Monsieur Alfonse took us there in his small hearse with the small horse and the big taxi-meter. As an inspiration to the others I chose to sit right up at the front, out in the open. Away from the smell of embalming fluid.

'We think the safe is in a room on the first floor,' Michelle briefed me as she handed forward the camera which was disguised as a potato. 'Deliver the food to the kitchen. Go to the room quickly. Photograph the safe and run like the clappers.'

'The last bit will be easy,' I said. I sometimes find that a little quip like this can do wonders for the troops' morale. 'But what do I say if I get caught?' Not for the first time, I felt it my job as commander to draw up a contingency plan that would buy valuable time for the others in the event of my capture.

'Say you are going to a Bring-Your-Own-Potato party.'

Really, that girl will be the death of us all. That is, if the RAF don't get there first. Leclerc intercepted us at that point to say he'd received a message on the wireless that they were going to bomb the German troops in Nouvion. To Edith this was excellent news. She said I should be proud to be bombed by them. Little did she realise, we are not insured against the RAF.

'Go back and tell them to keep well clear of the café,' I told the old fool. 'Tell them we will shine a torch up the chimney.'

No sooner had we arrived back in town than the British raid went ahead. If only they had known that in the pocket of the bravest man in all France was a potato containing a camera containing a picture of a safe containing the plans for the German invasion of England they would probably have tried not to hit me.

Unfortunately they did not know this. Perhaps, I thought, I should try to signal to them with my torch.

'Put out that lit or you will be shat on the spit,' shouted a policeman.

'Officer Crabtree,' I pleaded, 'can you not explain to your English friends that we are on their side? If I am killed it will be the end of the Resistance in this part of France.' Well, certainly in the doorway where I was standing.

RAF BOMB

BALL- BEARING FACTORY

Germans claim 43 Brits shot down – but we find no trace

'All pieces picked up very quickly' says Von Klinkerhoffen

'Bummers show plenty of fart left in earmen' says police eyewitness

In last night's massive raid by RAF bombers on the German ball-bearing factory at Nouvion, only two local casualties have so far been reported. One worker who lost his bearings, and another who lost his b

'You should be grateful that the RAF bummers are still farting for freedom,' he said.

There's not a lot you can say to that, is there?

15 OCTOBER

The old undertaker with the dicky ticker has developed the film in his embalming fluids and the old fool Leclerc has identified the make of the safe. I briefed Michelle to come up with a plan to get us into Gruber's room tonight so Leclerc can carry out a blow-job.

Michelle decided it would be a good idea to drop a smokebomb down Gruber's chimney. This will cause him to vacate the room. I hope that's all the scare will cause him to vacate. I will then smash in his window disguised as a fireman and enter with the geriatric geligniter, Leclerc – also disguised as a fireman.

Before I had time to comment on this brilliant stratagem, the idiot Crabtree arrived. He was walking very gingerly. 'I am sorry that I am lit,' he said, 'I had to wik curfully down the stroot because I have five fit of fuse wound round my log, and detonators dingling down my troosers.'

*Roger and out,
your loving son
Fairfax*

P.S Please tell Nanny my bowels are open again.

Needless to say, Michelle's masterplan blew up in her face.
Or rather, my face. She and Edith dropped the smokebomb
down the wrong chimney, and when I smashed my way
into Gruber's bedroom there wasn't a puff in sight, apart
from Gruber. Luckily, the General burst into the room at
this moment and shouted 'Fire!'

Crabtree was on hand to give some expert advice.
'Depress the plinger and direct the nizzle at the muddle of
the fear.'

'Get out of my way,' said Michelle as she pushed
Gruber aside. 'I can spray this only once.'

Leclerc and I escaped from the château in Gruber's
uniform and longcoat. We'd made it all the way back to
the café when we saw Germans outside. Luckily there was
a covered lorry to hide in until they went away. Unluckily,
the lorry was full of members of the Communist
Resistance.

'Oh, good evening,' I said pleasantly. 'You girls are
probably wondering why we are dressed as German
officers.'

'All German officers dress this way. Your French
accent does not fool us for one moment. Put up your
hands.'

'Look, you have got the wrong idea. We are French.
Just go into the little café in there and ask.'

'Café René?' their leader spat. 'We are the Communist
Resistance. We would not set foot in the café of that
collaborator dog who entertains the Germans every night.'

'One day we will shoot him and hang his body from a
lamp post,' said another. 'Now don't waste our time. What
is your name?'

'Captain Von Smittelhoffen,' I replied.

'Excuse me,' said Leclerc, 'will you also shoot his
pianist?'

'Of course.'

'Erich Von Beckstein at your service.'

ar Mumsy

Had another crack at giving ourselves up today, but the Krauts
st aren't playing ball.

ent up to a Jerry officer and used some of that German I learnt
school. "Mein Herr," I said, "Vee the British airmen are. Give up
y much we would like to."

you know what, Mumsy? The blighter swiped me on the knuckles with
cane. Just like old Stinky Blenkinsop used to when he took my
users down in his study. Flaming Krauts. Don't even understand
r own language. I tell you, Mumsy, if I wasn't writing to you
st and therefore had a stamp left I'd jolly well write to Hitler and tell
n what an absolute shower he's got here.

ll, chin up old thing. We're not going back to that froggie ca
r tails between our legs, I can tell you. We'd look a couple of rig
ar lies. Carstairs has had the wizard idea of commiting a crime and
 uing up to it. He's such a brick.

at sort of crime?" I asked him.

ell, how about chucking a brick through a shop window" he said.
right." I said, "off you go"

t the brick missed the window Mumsy and hit a Jerry on the
met. I don't think that's a crime we'll own up to.

TFN – must scarper

ger and out,
          Your loving son
                    Fairfax

P.S Please tell Nanny my bowels are open again.

17 OCTOBER

It was Michelle who broke the sad news of my capture to Edith, Yvette and Mimi. By all accounts they took it very hard.

'Where are they holding him?' asked Yvette.

'That's rather a personal question,' Michelle replied.

'I am his wife,' said Edith, 'you can tell me. Where are they holding him?'

'In the old saw-mill east of Nouvion.'

'We will storm the saw-mill and rescue him,' said Mimi.

'Yes, we will storm the saw-mill and rescue him,' said Edith. 'How will we rescue him?'

'Outside is Gruber's little tank. We will steal it. If necessary we will use the big gun and blow them to pieces.'

'But they are Frenchmen,' Yvette protested.

'They are the wrong Frenchmen.'

'It is a good plan,' said Michelle. 'Go quickly.'

'Are you not coming?'

'I cannot – I have a dinner party for the Rouen Resistance. The stew is in the oven.'

And so it was that the three of them launched themselves in Gruber's little tank on a rescue mission to save the bravest man in all France, reversed into the new town pissoir, and nearly killed the policeman who was swinging his truncheon in one of the cubicles.

'There is obviously no piss for the wicked,' he said as he rose unsteadily from the wreckage.

Luckily I did not need their help to escape. I have been released and this is how easy it was: Denise Laroque, the former lion-tamer and now leader of the fanatical Communist Resistance, Nouvion West Sub-Area, was just about to whip my naked back when she spotted the perfect strawberry birthmark – even to the little stalk – that I acquired when I was born in a snowstorm and the doctor could not come out because he had Asian 'flu so Madame Triconfort, who was my mother's daily help, assisted at

CAFÉ RENÉ

Dear friends in Avignon,

~~the town I should never have left~~, if you could see me now,
would weep for a poor old starving woman.

...to eat, I must pick camembert from the mousetraps with
...zers. The mice are living better in my daughter's cafe then her
...old starving mother. All she brings me is gruel made from potatoe
...s and chicken bones. I would cry with self-pity into this soup, but
...weak enough already.

René has gone on a mission and has not returned. Do not weep,
...ear friends in Avignon, the town I should never have left, he was
...thless bum. My daughter should marry that undertaker now
...e is bananas about her.

"But he is too old," Edith tells me. She thinks only of herself. What
...t my funeral? If she married him I could have a marble angel on
...mb blowing a trumpet. I have the inscription all ready:

> "How sad we are Mama's departed,
> But we remember how she
> From her birth destined for Heaven,
> Now she's gone at ninety-seven."

...now I am only ninety-five, but never fear, I am hanging on
...ake it rhyme.

Your poor old starving friend

Fanny

Dear Mumsy,

Rather put my foot in it today, I'm afraid. We went to the Froggie police station and gave ourselves up to a Froggie officer who had his back turned to us at the time.

"We British airmen come from sky." I said in English, but loud enough for the Froggie to understand. "Shot down, with to give up."

"Are you mad?" he said, turning round. "It is every officer's duty to escape."

Good heavens, Mumsy, it was Crabtree, the British agent. Fairfax took a firm line with him at once. "Now listen, weren't you sent to get us back to England?"

"Well it's very difficult, don't you know there's a war on?" I thought I'd put in my tuppence worth while we were at it: "We've been here for ages and nothing seems to happen."

"Well to be perfectly honest," said Crabtree, "we're not all satisfied with these De Gaulle Resistance people and we're thinking of taking our business elsewhere. The Communists seem to have more go in them."

Communists. Can you imagine it Mumsy? I said it would cost Daddy his seat if word got out.

"Parliament?"

"Wimbledon."

"I say, haven't you got a Liberal Resistance?" asked Fairfax.

"Yes," said Crabtree, "but he's in bed with the flu."

And we're still here in rotten old Froggie land.

Your loving son

Carstairs

P.S. Photo attached.

the confinement and used the tongs that were in the coal-bucket.

'I have seen this before,' Denise said. 'It was on the shoulder of my childhood sweetheart ... It was a hot August day on a riverbank in Nancy. The scent of the flowers in the field filled the air that we breathed. He was fishing. I sat beside him. He let me hold his worms. We kissed a tender kiss and the ice-cream that I was holding melted on his shirt.'

'Chocolate ripple,' I recalled.

'Correct. He removed his shirt to cleanse it in the bubbling stream and for the first time I saw the mark – this mark. But his name was René Artois.'

'My name is René Artois ...'

From that moment, everything fell into place. I was able to explain all my brave exploits that I have carried out so cleverly under the guise of a cowardly café-owner, and we were in the clear.

There is only one problem though. Denise Laroque has decided that destiny has thrown us together. The Welfare Committee of the Communist Resistance has had a meeting. By a show of daggers they have decided that she will be allowed to marry me and the wedding can take place on Saturday.

'We will commandeer the church of St Paul in the Rue de Vallee. We will kidnap the priest and we will break into the dress-shop of Madame Lenare and steal the wedding dress which is displayed in her window. For you, a wedding suit and top hat will be acquired by forcing the back door of the five-hundred-franc tailors in the High Street.'

It seems all the normal things have been taken care of. Who will be doing the catering, I wonder – or will it just be sandwiches on the run?

'You have a good week blowing things up and we'll meet at the church on Saturday,' I said to her.

A sixth sense tells me Edith is not going to be happy about all this.

18 OCTOBER

It appears from what Yvette tells me that several plots are being hatched by those who love and adore me to save me from the clutches of the Communist Resistance.

'If René marries Denise Laroque,' Edith said to Michelle, 'he will join the Communist Resistance and you will lose the services of the bravest man in all France.'

'I agree. He is our hero. We made him. The credit must not go to the loony left.'

'I have a plan,' my wife went on. 'Denise will be stealing her bridal gown from the dress shop of Madame Lenare. It is the one in the window with the thick veil. While she is doing this your people must kidnap her. I will take her place at the altar. Once René is married to me she can never wed him, because despite being a ruthless, murdering, bombing blackmailer, she is a good Catholic.'

Needless to say, I am to be kept in complete ignorance of this ...

21 OCTOBER

Edith walked into the bathroom while I was shaving this morning. No problem, except that Yvette had just been giving me a message* and had shaving soap on her face.

'Why has that serving girl got on her face shaving soap?' my inquisitive little wife wanted to know.

'Edith,' I said, 'have you no feelings? This poor shy slip of a girl has in her veins strong peasant blood. As a result

---

*   *A prime example of just how vigilant an editor must be. In René's original handwriting, this word might easily have been mistaken for 'massage', which of course would have made no sense at all. It is quite obvious that what happened was that my mother delivered a message from the Resistance that was so secret, she had to whisper it in René's ear. In the process, she ended up with shaving soap on her face – and a free shave from Edith into the bargain.*

of this she grows a moustache every three months. This has hitherto been kept a secret. You come blundering in and in twenty-four hours the whole village will hold her up to ridicule.'

'Oh René, I swear I will say nothing. Poor child. René, give me the razor, you have missed a bit ...'

22 OCTOBER

Imagine my surprise tonight when instead of opening the café as usual Edith laid on a little surprise for me. Yvette told me why she had done so later in the larder when we were canning noodles.*

'I have prepared for him to have a romantic candlelit dinner,' Edith had said to her and Mimi. 'It is for me to say to him one last fond farewell before he marries another.'

'It is terrible,' Yvette agreed. 'With that Laroque woman he will be dead within one week.'

'Unless the bullets get him first,' said Mimi.

I was taken aback to see Edith appear in such a nice dress. 'Does this mean you are to try out a new cabaret on your unsuspecting public?' I asked. But Edith led me into the back room. The table was set with candles, and there were many flowers and cards.

'See, there are candles, there are flowers,' she said. 'You know what this means?'

'Your mother is dead.'

'No, do you not recall? This is just how the table was set for dinner the first night of our honeymoon. I have planned that we should end our life together just as we started it.'

---

* *A pity about the smudged ink on these words. At first glance they appear to be saying 'canoodling', but it is clear to me that the correct interpretation is the one I have chosen to print, which concerns food preparation in the cellar.*

'We are not committing suicide, are we?'

'You are overwrought, René,' said Edith, and she was right.

As I sat down, she handed me the napkin as she had done that night. On the table were all the cards that our friends had sent to us to wish us good luck and happiness.

'Now,' Edith said, 'a little wine. It is the same wine

As René himself often said: 'Give me the tool and I'll finish the job.'

that we drank that night.'

'Ah, lucky we remembered to put the cork back in.'

Then it all started to come back to me in a tidal wave of memories. Edith was sixteen, the prettiest looking girl in the street. Come to think of it, she was the only girl in the street.

'Dear Edith, you are very sweet. I do not deserve you – perhaps I never did. Here I am about to marry another and you are being so brave. You are reminding me of all the things about you that I shall miss. You have arranged everything as it was all those years ago. The flowers, the candles, the table – all as it was in that little private room in that little hotel.'

'And there is one other thing that is the same ...'

'The bill?'

'No.' She rang a little bell. In came her mother, dressed as a Nippy girl waitress. It was not the most erotic of sights.

'Oh yes, I forgot. Your mother got us a special rate because she worked there.'

The old crone poured us some soup.

'I have prepared the same menu,' said Edith. 'We dined, we drank, we talked, we went to bed in each other's arms and as the clock struck twelve ...'

'Consommé,' said her mother.

'No,' I said, 'not that night.'

Yvette and Mimi, bless them, have hatched a plot of their own. It involves interfering with the priest at my wedding.

I will not write any more. I must get my sleep. Tomorrow night is going to be one of the biggest of my life. I have a reputation for being the hardest man in all France. I only hope I can keep it up.

As I write this entry, dear Diary, Edith is over there at the window table gently weeping. The reason is as follows. When, yesterday afternoon, I was at the point of twenty guns in the process of marrying Denise Laroque, the Head of the Communist Resistance, Nouvion Division, Edith, bravely or stupidly, depending on your viewpoint, substituted herself for Denise in the hope of becoming my bride. Little did she know that my waitresses, who both

ARCH OF CROSSED DAGGERS AT NOUVION WEDDING

The wedding took place on Saturday afternoon of M. René Artois, the popular owner of the Café René, and Mme Denise Laroque, the fanatical ex-lion tamer, now leader of the Communist Resistance (Nouvion West Sub-Area).

The groom wore a traditional wedding suit with trousers that were tight under the arms. The bride was resplendent in a thick veil.

Best Man was Monsieur Alfonse. Those in attendance included: Colonel Von Strohm and Lieutenant Gruber (in plain clothes with bowler hats); many peasants; several pretty girls who were crying; many grim-faced girls of the Communist Resistance, and Michelle of the ordinary Resistance.

The bride walked down the aisle to the tune of the Red Flag, and as everyone is equal with the Communists, she gave herself away.

Specially present for the occasion was one of the Church's most senior clerics.

'We are gathered together in the presence of Gid,' he began, 'to jane this women and this min in Haly Weedlock.'

Apparently these Roman Catholic services are always conducted in Latin.

Organist: Monsieur Leclerc
Choir members included: Fraulein Helga Geerhart (mezzo soprano) Herr Otto Flick (sinister baritone). Chief Mourners: Mme Yvette, Mm Mimi.

have the hots for me, had substituted Crabtree the idiot English agent for the Catholic priest.*

This means of course that the wedding was not legal (a) because he was not a proper priest and (b) because even the good Lord himself could not have understood one word of the ceremony, which due to his atrocious French accent was fortunately presumed by Lieutenant Gruber and the other guests to be in Latin.

28 OCTOBER

My fanatical childhood sweetheart kills any man who rejects her. Who will she blame for this fiasco? Me – because I told everyone of the wedding plans. It is little consolation that she is apparently safely held up in the bottom of a mine shaft by Michelle of the Resistance. What happens if she escapes? How will I carry on the fight for liberty if I have been gunned down by a jealous ex-lover?

'We will keep her there until after the war,' says Edith. 'I will send sandwiches down.'

Yes, and with any luck they'll hit her on the head. A glancing blow from one of Edith's spam and lettuce doorsteps would give her something to think about all right. I should know, I was on the receiving end of one last year when Edith caught me on the billiard table showing Yvette how to go in off, and my actions were totally misinterpreted. I still needed massage a fortnight later.

'With your reputation, Monsieur, it will be assumed that she is too exhausted to resume guerrilla warfare,' said Monsieur Alfonse helpfully.

'What reputation?' Edith wanted to know.

'It is all part of the myth, Edith,' I tried to explain.

* It is an enigma to me why René should choose this moment to mention that both Yvette and Mimi appear to have successfully purchased for him a pair of heated hostess trolleys.

'Word of mouth exaggerates little things into big things.
I blow up a bus station, it becomes an ammunition factory.
You know how it is. But you are all to blame. Perhaps this
will teach you to consult me before putting into effect your
idiot plans.'

Just think, dear Diary. Denise Laroque has been
shafted! She will not like this. I can see her right now,
scraping at the earth with her bare hands, spitting my
name between clenched teeth. What happens if she finds
a shovel? Oh my God, I wish I hadn't thought of that.

'The mine shaft is a mile deep . . .' said Edith
comfortingly.

A mile deep. Is that all?

3 NOVEMBER

Michelle of the Resistance came to see me today and added
to my concern.

'What are you doing here?' I demanded. 'You should
be sitting on a big slab of stone on top of the mine shaft.'

'The slab of stone is still in place.'

'Thank heavens.'

'Unfortunately, Denise found a shovel.'

I knew it! Apparently she tunnelled into an adjacent
shaft, and though the guard followed her through a
labyrinth of tunnels and passages, she outpaced him and
fled, spitting my name through her clenched teeth.

'Oh my God. Well, that is it. Yvette – my hat and coat.'

I was going to give myself up to the Germans. It was
the only way to keep myself alive to fight for France
another day. I would tell them I stole their painting. They
would put me in jail, of course, but with good conduct I
should be out in a few years, by which time Denise would
with any luck have blown herself up.

But just as I was about to leave, the café door burst

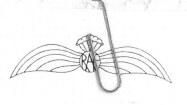

Dear Mumsy,

I am a caged lion. I can't stand being cooped up in a police station much longer. I have an idea running round my head – I'll rip it out and see what you think.

There's always a little tank parked outside the cafe. Why don't Carstairs and I dress up as Krauts and steal it? I drove Daddy's Austin Seven once. Must be the same principle. We could fight our way to the coast, bash into the docks, hijack a submarine and poodle across to England.

I hope you think more of the plan than Carstairs did. When I put it to him all he did was wish me good luck. Seems he's not coming with me.

Roger and out
Your loving son
Fairfax.

open. A girl with a machine gun leapt inside and sprayed the bar with bullets. I fell down behind the bar at once, stone dead.

Only pretending, of course. But since I'd managed to escape the bullets it seemed to make a lot of sense to stay where I was – lying under Yvette and Mimi.

I have spent the rest of the day disguised as my own father, seeking asylum from the Germans, the Gestapo and the gendarmes.

'The fanatical head of the Communist Resistance is trying to kill me!' I said to the Colonel and Lieutenant Gruber.

'You will get used to it,' said the Colonel. 'They are trying to kill us all the time.'

Herr Flick of the Gestapo did not exactly embrace the role of protector with open arms, either.

'Could you not keep me in a dungeon for a few days until the heat is off?' I pleaded.

'*We* pick the people we lock up,' he said.

And as for the gendarmerie! I went there and rang the bell for several minutes before a policeman appeared.

'Will you please stop bonging the bill,' he said. 'Or I shall lick you up for disturbing the puss. Are you confessing to some cream? In that curse you must fill in a foam.'

But it turned out that all the cills were filled to copocity anyway. My only hope would be to come back next woke. Oh my God. Why do I pay rates?

I got back to the café only to find myself the victim of a poisoned wine attack by the Communist Resistance. It was the final straw. I resolved to head at once for the station. Until the dust settles here, there must be a vacancy for a cuckoo clock salesman in Switzerland.

I left the café a desperate man. The next thing I knew, I was being escorted into the back of a Communist Resistance lorry to be reunited with my erstwhile bride, Denise Laroque.

'I know the truth,' she said. Much to my surprise she did not spit, as she spoke, through clenched teeth. 'In a fit of pique I tried to have you shot only to discover that you were blameless. It is the women of the café that I should kill.'

'Well, of course, it was their fault, but is killing not a little drastic? I am sure they would apologise, pay you nominal damages.'

Denise's response was to grab me and crush her lips against mine. She made me swear that I will never leave her again. I swore.

'Now – I have bad news,' she added. 'I must go to Lyon for the party conference. I have been nominated to be Party Chairman.'

'Oh dear,' I sighed, 'can you not get out of it?'

'No,' she said firmly. 'All is ready for me. The ballots have been rigged. The moderates are under lock and key. The democratic process must take its course. But I will return for revenge – and for love.'

I can hardly wait.

5 NOVEMBER

I have had to break the bad news to the women in my life that they are on the hit list of the fanatical Denise Laroque. She has vowed to kill them all. Edith first.

Edith did not take it well.

'Right, that is it,' she said, going to the till and taking out all the money. 'The Spanish border cannot be that far away. If I walk all night and crawl all day I could be there by Christmas.'

'Edith, you will never get to the end of the street. The Communists have gun-persons everywhere.'

'Then I will disguise myself.'

And that was the last I have seen of her. Maybe there's something to be said for Karl Marx after all.

8 NOVEMBER

Michelle of the Resistance stole up my back passage again tonight and crept into the kitchen just as I was showing Yvette how I like to have my b ls fond ed.*

    'Michelle,' I said, 'it is not always convenient to have you barging in on my private moments. Could you not make an appointment?'

* *Another smudged entry that might be open to possible misinterpretation. The correct reading, however, since they are in the kitchen, appears to be that René is instructing Yvette as to how he likes to have his 'bols fondued'. I have been unable to trace any other reference in Normandy cookery books to what must be a peculiarly regional dish featuring the fiery Dutch liqueur, but it certainly sounds as though it would make your mouth water.*

'The German Generals will soon be meeting at the château to discuss plans for the invasion of England,' she carried on. 'Their maps will be on the table. Somehow we must photograph them.'

'Why are you telling me this?'

'Because you will be asked to do the catering.'

'How do you know?' I asked. 'There are three other catering firms in Nouvion.'

'Yours will be the lowest estimate or else the others will be burned down for collaborating.'

11 NOVEMBER

Poor Herr Flick. Helga tells me he has placed an advertisement in the local paper for a servant but he has had only one reply. It came through the window on a brick.

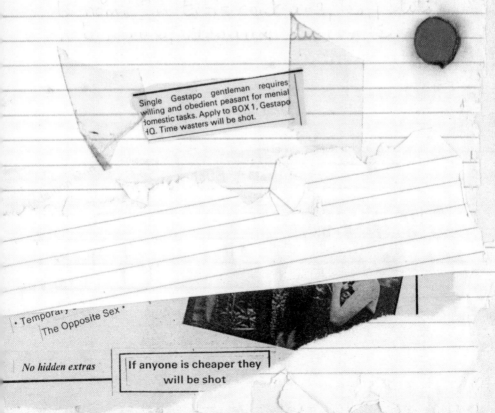

Single Gestapo gentleman requires willing and obedient peasant for menial domestic tasks. Apply to BOX 1, Gestapo HQ. Time wasters will be shot.

* Temporary *
The Opposite Sex *

No hidden extras

If anyone is cheaper they will be shot

12 NOVEMBER

Would you believe it possible that the British have scaled new heights of madness?

Michelle burst into the back room this morning just as I was having a tiff with Mimi.*

'The RAF have dropped the bird that will carry the photographs back to England,' she said. 'It will be delivered today.'

'Well, for heaven's sake label it,' I said. 'My wife cooked the last pigeon for lunch.'

'It is not a pigeon. The Germans are shooting them down.'

'Then what is it?'

'It is a long-distance duck.'

'Now I have heard everything. Is this duck expected to fly all the way to England?'

'Should it become exhausted it will land on the English Channel and have a sleep. For this reason the photographs will be in waterproof containers.'

See what I mean?

---

* *A reader less schooled in the character and ways of René Artois than I might easily be under the misguided impression here that instead of saying 'having a tiff' this partly smudged sentence actually says: 'having it off'. This is, of course, not only a blatantly outrageous suggestion, but a sickeningly unpatriotic one too. Just what the tiff was about, however, we are never told – testimony, surely, to René's outstanding powers of discretion when it comes to matters of staff relations.*

OTTO FLICK

Gestap-o-grams

Sinister Grams for Special Occasions

* Boobiegrams * **Nurses** *
* **Full strip** * Nuns
* Jockeys

Spanking Schoolgirls

* Traffic Wardens
* **Leathermen**
* Vicars *
* Naughty Hitler Youths

* **Secret Policemen** *

Heinrich Himmler Lookalikes * Bride & Leather Girls * * **Cowboys** Maids *

* Medallion Men * Flashers

* **White Rabbits** * **Male SS Strippers**

* **Rubber Girls** * * Tarzans

* **Drunken Scots** * **Gorillas**

Casanovas *

* Temporary Stenographers Of The Opposite Sex *

No hidden extras

If anyone is cheaper they will be shot

14 NOVEMBER

The Colonel wants to rescue the real paintings from their hiding place at the headquarters of the Communist Resistance. The Communists were armed to the teeth, I told him. They would be very dangerous.

'Could you not mount a military operation?' Helga asked. 'Say a company of infantry, some artillery and a few tanks, with a token amount of air cover?'

'No. The General might ask questions. We will have to be more sneaky than that – perhaps using only a handful of carefully selected ruthless men.'

'Providing we can find them!' quipped Lieutenant Gruber.

This comment drew a black look from the Colonel, but Gruber's bacon was saved by the entry at that moment of the Itie with the turkey feathers in his hat.

'Colonel-o, your old buddy Alberto Bertorelli is-a returned from Roma. See here – Mussolini, he give me a beautiful medal. In Roma I am given the finest crack troops in all-a Italy. Together we take-a the boats and we invade the British. I pick-a my men – each one with my own-a hand. They are the ruthless men.'

'Ruthless men?' I said. 'With respect, Colonel, I think this may be the answer to your problem ...'

'When can we meet them?' the Colonel asked.

'They wait-a for you to make-a the inspection. Come outside and say hallo.'

Outside in the town square were some of the scruffiest long-haired layabouts I have ever seen assembled in one place since Nouvion were at home to Port Vale in a pre-war friendly.* A complete shower. A shambles.

'Men, pay attention,' Gruber addressed the mob. 'I am Lieutenant Gruber – that is my little tank.'

'Oh – nice-a tank! Pretty!'

* *Nouvion won 3–0.*

'We have an assignment for you. North-east of this town is the headquarters of the Communist Resistance. We have important documents to recover from them. They are armed to the teeth and, like you, they are ruthless, desperate fighters.'

'To you will go the honour of attacking and defeating them,' said the Colonel.

'This is a great honour,' said Bertorelli. 'What do you say boys? Can-a we do it!'

To a man, the Ities scattered. Where once had stood the pride of Italy in their wide variety of ill-fitting uniforms, there was now only a pile of badly packed kit bags, half-eaten pizzas and a jar of Brylcreem.

Men after my own heart, I say.*

18 NOVEMBER

The German Generals begin their week-long meeting in the château tomorrow. They will be planning the invasion of England. The Resistance needs photographs of the maps.

'Michelle,' I enquired selflessly, 'this time, wouldn't you like to take the glory?'

'There will be no danger,' she said. 'We have devised a special apparatus which will not be visible.'

Oh yes, this apparatus will not be visible. Do you know what it consists of? A sort of jacket affair, with a false left arm that rests on the hip. This is to leave my left hand free to operate my apparatus. With the jacket is also an apron, beneath which is a camera.

---

* René appears to have misinterpreted the Italians' response. He is under the impression that they – as the bravest man in all France would have done in their place – have rushed off at once to carry out their deadly task. It would not have occurred to such a gallant fighter that the Italians had simply scarpered.

The TATE GALLERY

VAN CLOMP
RETROSPECTIVE

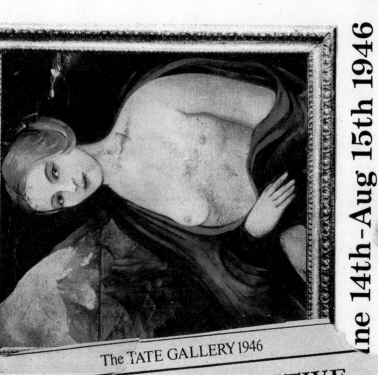

The TATE GALLERY 1946

VAN CLOMP RETROSPECTIVE

The Van Clomp retrospective now showing for a limited season at the Tate Gallery offers a rare opportunity to re-assess this artist's unique features.

In any exhibition of Van Clomp's work, his extraordinary Fallen Madonna with the Big Boobies must inevitably provide the centrepieces. The eye is constantly drawn back to this canvas by the boldness of the brushstrokes, the sheer enormity of the vision. But it should not, nay cannot, obscure our appreciation of the other paintings assembled here for the first time by the Argentine-based fine art emporium of Gruber Geering Von Strohm.

True, certain basic themes are re-stated in La Madone Tombée avec les Boobies Grandes, and indeed in Zu Madonna mit das Grosses Boobies Gefallen. On closer inspection, however, the connoisseur will notice slight differences between the twelve or so works on display – subtle nuances of shade and line, of shape and colour, that can only enhance one's sense of wonder.

It is hardly surprising that they have been so long sought after, nor that they have without exception fallen into the hands of private collectors.

'How am I supposed to operate it?' I asked.

'Feel around and you will find a little knob. Have you got it?'

'I think so.'

'Pull it.'

I did. A small panel in the front of the apron lifted up, revealing a small camera and lens. There was a flash, then it disappeared again.

'Just think, René – with this you can save the world.'

I was speechless. If the future of civilisation as we know it depends upon the success of this device, is it a civilisation that is worth saving?

20 NOVEMBER

Leclerc has brought bad news. As he opened the hen-house door, the duck flew away. But he thinks he will not go far. He has not had his lunch.

Alfonse might save the day. He has duck-hunting equipment. Apparently, he used to stand in the river with an artificial duck on his head. Between his teeth he would hold his duck-quacker. He says that in his time he was famous for it. I am not surprised.

22 NOVEMBER

Alfonse and Leclerc spent the morning in the re-built pissoir together, with artificial ducks on their heads.

'Monsieur,' Leclerc asked Alfonse, 'why are we quacking here in the public convenience?'

'Because if the long-distance duck sees our bodies he will be put off. This way he will think we are two lady ducks. He will fly down and I will capture him with my fish-landing net.'

They were joined at this moment by the Itie, Bertorelli.

'Excusa that I ask,' said the Itie, 'but why do you wear on your head a duck?'

'We are trying to capture the duck that is quacking up

OCCUPIED
COUNTRY LIFE

VOL. XXXVIII   OCTOBER 1941

Fraulein Helga Geerhart, only daughter of Herr and Frau Herman Geerhart of Stuttgart, who is engaged to be married to Herr Otto Flick, whose family background is very exalted and is nobody's business.

there,' said Alfonse.

'For our dinner,' added Leclerc.

'Ah – I see. That a piece-a cake-a.'

And with that he took out his revolver and fired a shot into the sky. Out of the sky thudded a duck.

'Have a good dinner,' said Bertorelli.

24 NOVEMBER

I am taking pills to calm my nerves. I need them for many reasons. First, because I have just photographed the map of the German plan to invade England.

Also, because Lieutenant Gruber has just cruised in on a social call and he's wearing the perfume that is so popular with the Tank Corps, lily of the valley with a hint of diesel oil. By the glint in his eye, I'd say his sights were firmly set on opening up a second front before the night is out. I'm very keen that it shouldn't be mine.

The Resistance are at this moment developing the negatives in Monsieur Alfonse's embalming fluid. Fortunately, the Itie Bertorelli had missed the duck, but the poor animal collapsed out of the sky with shock. Now it is lying in a basket suffering from feather fatigue. It is in no condition to fly to England. I thought it best to take its temperature a few moments ago, so I shook the thermometer and shoved it into the duck's basket.

'It may have interrupted a nice dream,' said Edith with concern.

'It has probably started one,' I said.

'Come to think of it,' said the Lieutenant, 'I'm beginning to feel a little feverish myself.'

ar Mumsy,

You know, the flood here is absolutely
's a complete myth about French cooking being
best in the world, and the fact that we're in
l is no excuse. All you can taste is garlic. If we
ght one of the rats we could probably barbecue it
r a candle.

Do you know, Mumsy, I've been thinking – it's about
e those Americans came in. They saved us in the
t war. If they don't hurry up there won't be any
r left.

Fairfax is a bit down in the mouth again. He
s if his mummy and daddy knew he was in jail they'd
e a fit. I've told him not to worry – it's not going
be in the Tatler, is it? He's worried that if it ever
mes out that he's got a prison record it could stop
m getting a decent job after the war. I asked him
shat he's going to do and he says he's going into
he Stock Exchange, so that's all right isn't it – they won't
ind.

Well, must go now to bribe a guard or someone to
smuggle this out for me.

Roger and out,
Your loving jailbird (ha.ha.!) son,

Carstairs

P.S. Will the garlic be all right for my spots Mumsy?
I don't want the other boys laughing at me when
I get back to the squadron.
P.P.S. Photo attached.

25 NOVEMBER

Today I resigned from the Resistance. I am no longer a member. If Michelle thinks I'm incompetent just because I took a photograph of a map that the Germans hadn't yet marked she can take her duck and her radio and find someone else to be the bravest man in all France.

26 NOVEMBER

Today I am back in the Resistance. Last night Michelle slipped secretly up my back passage and refused to accept my resignation.

'I cannot go on without you,' she said. 'I love you. I always have and until the end of time I always will.'

So that is settled. After talks lasting just under two hours in the back room, I put my major point on the table and pushed it home hard. Michelle seemed quietly impressed. I have now seen everything from another angle. I am back in my old position.*

28 NOVEMBER

Lieutenant Gruber and two stormtroopers popped into the café tonight, with orders to arrest me. General Von Klinkerhoffen thinks that I am responsible for trying to poison everyone at the Generals' meeting at the château. Hence I am writing this in the cupboard in the bedroom of my wife's mother. In the dark. It seems imperative to me that the Resistance is not deprived of its leader at this

* *We'll probably never know the exact nature of René's negotiating instrument, nor the full scope of his demands. Knowing René, money alone would not have come into it. Far more likely is that he was hanging out for improved satisfaction on the job.*

crucial stage of the war. My one regret about going into
hiding is the terrible smell that seems to hang around this
room, like stale onion soup. Perhaps a mouse has died.

29 NOVEMBER

I am going to make a run for it, disguised as a French
General with a big hooter. Leclerc has modelled me one
out of plastic explosive. It will not go off unless I light the
wick, which is buried in my nostril. Thank heavens I do not
smoke. Or pick my nose.

To create a diversion in the café Yvette is going to
tempt the Colonel upstairs with a special end-of-season
offer – wet rhubarb. This will enable me to walk out of the
front door, turn left, and head for Spain. My fondest hope
is that I'll be able to maintain my affairs from such a long
distance away. And that Yvette will understand why it
was essential for me to pull out so early.

30 NOVEMBER

I gave Yvette one last fond embrace in the cellar this
morning and walked upstairs. Unfortunately, the Colonel
and Gruber were waiting at the bar.

'Ah, General!' called the Colonel. 'How good to see you.
Come to our table and take some wine. It is so good to
have you on our side.'

'I am sorry, Colonel, I cannot,' I said. 'I have an urgent
appointment to do some collaborating.'

'Colonel,' he said, 'it is René under an assumed nose.'

Unfortunately the assumed nose was tickling me, and
I sneezed. I didn't realise that the wick was then left
dangling from my nostril, and everyone was too polite to
tell me. The three of us put our heads together
conspiratorially over the candle to discuss the paintings

of The Fallen Madonna with the Big Boobies by Van Clomp
and the Cracked Vase with the Big Daisies by Van Gogh.

'René,' the Colonel said, 'your nose is smouldering.'

Oh my God! Seizing the nose with both hands, I tore it
off and ran to the door of the café. Edith opened it and I
threw the highly explosive hooter out into the street in the
nick of time. There was the sound of a big explosion.

'I apologise for my mother,' said Edith to the Colonel.
'She is ninety-five, you know.'

But just then Herr Flick appeared at the door. His
leather coat and hat were in tatters and his stick was
splayed. He took just two paces inside the café, spun on
one heel and passed out.

2 DECEMBER

Lieutenant Gruber has informed General Von
Klinkerhoffen that a French General attempted to
assassinate Herr Flick of the Gestapo by exploding him.
He now suspects the Vichy official of being the miscreant
who tried to kill everyone at the meeting in the château.
The finger of suspicion therefore no longer points at me.
I am a free man!

'Whatever you want here will be on the house,
Lieutenant,' said Edith.

'As long as it is on the menu,' I added.

Herr Flick is recovering in bed in his cellar. His arm is
in a splint and tied to the roof in a 'Heil Hitler' position.
One leg is suspended on a pulley.

Helga tells me she went to visit him a little earlier.

'It is terrible to see you like this, Herr Flick,' she said.
'Has any vital organ received damage?'

'I am testing them one at a time,' he replied.

4 DECEMBER

You may be wondering, dear Diary, why it is that you are down in the cellar of my café and why I am bricking myself up. I will tell you. Last night ten German Generals were planning the invasion in my café. To avoid being blown up by the Resistance they were disguised as French onion-sellers. Unfortunately they became mixed up with a lot of British airmen, also, of course, disguised as French onion-sellers. Thanks to the Resistance they are now on their way to the coast in a fish-truck to be taken by submarine to England. Naturally I will be blamed, so I intend to remain down here behind this wall till after the war.

5 DECEMBER

Edith has brought me two bottles of my favourite cognac and some more baked beans.

'Edith, I already have eight cases of baked beans – have you nothing else?'

'Here is a gorgonzola and some candles.'

'I think in the circumstances it will be better if they remain unlit.'

6 DECEMBER

Edith now wants to join me. She says that if the Germans can't find me, they will blame her. Yvette thinks that if the Germans can't find Edith, they will blame her. She, too, wants to join me.

'There is not enough room!' Edith protested. 'We will have to sleep on top of each other.'

'We must not be selfish, Edith,' I said.

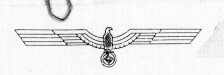

TO: HERR OTTO FLICK
FROM: GESTAPO LOVED ONES' ANTI-HANKY-PANKY DEPARTMENT

TRANSCRIPT OF CONVERSATION BETWEEN LIEUTENANT HUBERT GRUBER
THE SUSPECT, PRIVATE HELGA GEERHART, RECORDED BY POWERFUL GE
LISTENING DEVICE NO. 443/D, WHICH IN THE OFFICE OF THE SECRE
OF COLONEL VON STROHM IS LOCATED.

SUSPECT: I have just made some coffee. Would you like some
GRUBER: You are most kind. Very few people are kind to me
          the moment. I find this most touching.
SUSPECT: You look pale Lieutenant.
GRUBER: Well, I'm not really cut out for all this war like
          activity you know. True, I have some affection fo
          little tank but I don't wish to become attached to
          I will have to hand it back when the war is over,
          I not?
SUSPECT: We all have to find what consolation we can in our
          unfamiliar roles. Take me for instance. The mate
          of my uniform has a coarse and unyielding texture
          I find it quite erotic. Unfortunately when it rai
          colour runs all over my underwear.
GRUBER: I miss the carefree life of a window dresser. It
          wonderful. I could position the models exactly as
          wished. Then I could watch the passers-by press t
          noses to the glass. Sometimes when I had finished
          would applaud.
SUSPECT: Have courage, Lieutenant Gruber. There will be wi
          after the war.
GRUBER: Not many.

7 DECEMBER

First the good news. The fish-lorry hit a bomb crater and all the German Generals are on their way back to Berlin. Now at least they will not know that they were being driven to the coast to be shipped off to England. They will simply think they were being driven to safety from the air-raid.

Now for the bad news. Gruber tells me that Berlin is blaming General Von Klinkerhoffen for the whole fiasco and General Von Klinkerhoffen is blaming the Colonel. The Colonel is bound to look for a scapegoat. I'm not absolutely sure what a scapegoat looks like, but I expect he will have a moustache, be slightly thinning on top, and will run a pleasant café in the Nouvion area of Normandy.

11 DECEMBER

Lieutenant Gruber came into the café in some distress tonight. He arrived in his little tank as usual, but I could tell by the grinding of the gears that he was out of sorts. It is not like him to have trouble finding reverse.

'It's a rather special friend, René ... he has been badly wounded.'

'That's terrible, Lieutenant. Where was he hit?'

'In the Bulge.'

'Very painful. Can I be of any assistance?'

'Thank you, René. Just lend me your support.'

'Of course, Lieutenant. Borrow *both* my supports if you think they will help ...'

14 DECEMBER

The Colonel wants the Itie Bertorelli to help him and Gruber escape to Italy. With his connections in Rome they can arrange to hide out in the Vatican. But it will take money. Lots of money. The sort of money you can only raise by selling paintings of The Fallen Madonna with the Big Boobies by Van Clomp and the Cracked Vase with the Big Daisies by Van Gogh.

'What about Helga?' Lieutenant Gruber asked the Colonel. 'We promised to cut her in.'

'We will cut her out. They do not like women at the Vatican.'

'Is there any chance of getting there for Christmas?' the Lieutenant said.

15 DECEMBER

Lieutenant Gruber tells me that the Itie Bertorelli has his doubts about the Colonel's plan.

'Colonel-o,' he said, 'I have to tell you that big boobies

```
                           ... The mate
                    - and unyielding texture
                 - erotic.  Unfortunately when it rai
            ...our runs all over my underwear.
GRUBER:    I miss the carefree life of a window dresser.  It w
           wonderful.  I could position the models exactly as
           wished.  Then I could watch the passers-by press th
           noses to the glass.  Sometimes when I had finished
           would applaud.
SUSPECT:   Have courage, Lieutenant Gruber.  There will be win
           after the war.
GRUBER:    Not many.
```

cut no ice with the Pope.'

Michelle, of course, has other ideas. 'The Resistance need the paintings to sell for the Party funds,' she told me. 'You should take the forgeries, go to the headquarters of the Communist Resistance and substitute them so that the Germans will think that they have recovered the originals.'

'How could I do this? They have look-outs. Everyone who approaches will be shot.'

'They will not shoot a Franciscan friar wheeling a pram.'

Well, that would be an unusual sight, I had to admit. Especially with Mimi inside the pram dressed up as a baby. And even more so when the Franciscan friar wheeling his pram is shadowed at a distance of no more than a hundred metres or so by a mobile Gestapo observation unit consisting of Helga disguised as a nanny and Herr Flick curled up cosily inside with his gun in a dolly.

Resistance Weekly
Caption competition

"LISTEN VERY CAREFULLY, I SHALL SAY THIS ONLY ONCE."

"BAD NEWS FROM THE FRONT?"

"YOU COULD SAY THAT. ONE OF MY GIRLS HAS BEEN WOUNDED IN THE BREST AREA....."

This weeks winner- R. ARTOIS OF NOUVION

16 DECEMBER

Guess what popped out of the woodwork as soon as we had located the real paintings and swopped them over with the forgeries? Six highly-armed Communist girls and Denise Laroque, their highly-sexed leader.

'René Artois – my lover, my childhood sweetheart! You have returned to me as I knew that you would.'

'Hello,' I said. 'How was Lyon?'

She did not have a chance to tell me. At that moment shots rang out all around us. We were being stormed by Lieutenant Gruber in his little tank, with the Colonel, Edith, Yvette, Mimi and Monsieur Leclerc all in tow, and the Itie Bertorelli's hand-picked band of ruthless warriors. Seconds later, the white flag went up. Bertorelli had surrendered.

Any ideas on what I do next, dear Diary?

Here I am in the headquarters of the Communist Resistance, with no means of escape and everyone who might have come to my rescue also captured. All the paintings of The Fallen Madonna with the Big Boobies by Van Clomp and the Cracked Vase with the Big Daisies by Van Gogh are now in the hands of the Communists. The café is supposed to open at six and there is no one to run it. And as if all that wasn't enough, I've just run out of pages in this diary.*

---

* *It is perhaps just as well that René has run out of space. As my mother never tired of telling me, if the great man could be said to have had one outstanding feature it was a tendency to be over-length.*

  One cannot help wondering what the missing sections of his diary would have revealed, but one thing is beyond doubt – it can never be said that René Artois did not have a hard war.

GESTAPO INC.
BERLIN

From the desk of the M.D.

ar Otto,

am most displeased with your lack of progress. Hitler still
es not have the painting of the Fallen Madonna with the Big
obies which he promised to Eva for her birthday, and you have
ovided no evidence of the plot to blow up the Fuhrer. What
 more you have so far cost us two staff cars, one blown up a
e flattened by a steam-roller.

at sort of a Gestapo are you running up there? Get your act
gether or you could find yourself limping around the Russian
ont.

ur affectionate uncle,

INY

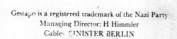

Gestapo is a registered trademark of the Nazi Party
Managing Director: H Himmler
Cables SINISTER BERLIN

HEADQUARTERS OF THE COMMUNIST RESISTANCE

NOUVION WEST SUB AREA

Comme vous pouvez voire Cher Journal,
il sera quelque changes ici à
l'avenir.

As you can see, Comrade Diary, there are going to be a few changes around here from now on.

'ALLO 'ALLO!

THE COMPLETE WAR DIARIES OF RENÉ ARTOIS

VOLUME 2

INTRODUCTION

T he successful publication of the first volume of *The War Diaries of René Artois* has unleashed an appetite amongst readers of discrimination which must be satisfied.

I myself confess to having become considerably excited by the great man's revelations and, though I began by thinking that they would only afford me a light though tasty literary snack, I have now realised that we can make a meal of them.

Volume One, of course, was all over by Christmas 1941, but Yvette Carte Blanche, my mother, had often referred tantalisingly to René's many other entries. Thus I made it my business to unearth evidence of further memoirs. The search took me very far afield. From the bordellos of Trastèvre to the Auction Rooms of Buenos Aires I exerted myself tirelessly. Nonetheless, I still managed to find the energy to get to grips with a mature Christmas pudding that had been served to Yvette recently in the buffet car on the train from Nouvion to Paris. Recognising it immediately, she had brought it home concealed about her person. She assured me it contained something very explosive.

She was right. I prodded it gently with a fork. There was a big bang, and the pudding was blown all over the kitchen, along with several thousand words of the second volume of *The War Diaries of René Artois*. Sharp-sighted readers will realise this explains certain unfortunate gaps in the text which follows.

There is still cause for celebration, however. I was able to piece the manuscript painstakingly together, and found that I had much important archive material on my hands, not to mention my face and neck.

Despite Edith's best efforts, it is René's voice which once again unmistakably colours the text, along with a great many scorch-marks and morsels of pudding. But it is typical of the man's generosity that he very rarely stands alone. Many of the protagonists in this drama are given the chance to reveal themselves, and often in a startling light.

We continue to gain privileged access to Colonel Von Strohm's plans for the post-war art market, to the terrible instrument of torture lurking in Herr Flick's private quarters, and to General Von Klinkerhoffen's detailed preparations for Hitler's birthday.

We see a great deal of Helga, and slightly less of Mimi Labonq and Englebert Von Smallhausen (especially after one of the Nouvion church bells falls on him).

The volume also contains much evidence of René the visionary. My mother often told me that the great man was capable of huge leaps of the imagination, and rarely is this better illustrated than by his proposal for a *Blue Guide to Nouvion*, for which he intended to take personal responsibility. He foresaw a considerable increase in traffic through the entire region between '42 and '45, and aimed

to capitalise upon it. Excerpts from the guide, with maps and cross-sections, are dotted through the text.

We find ourselves on an intimate tour through what he liked to call Artois Country, stopping at the butcher's with the big chopper, Herr Flick's dungeon, Hubert Gruber's favourite positions and much more besides. Not for nothing had he penned the slogan which was to become a byword in the Nouvion market: '1942 – Open for Business.'

Amongst the charred pages of this historic document we also discover a surprise or two waiting in the hat shop of the girl with the big berets and, closer to home, the little cupboard under the stairs. Many critics have been puzzled by the variety and extent of the entertainment available in a town of such modest proportions but, as René himself said on more than one occasion, size is not everything. Also, this was before the advent of television.

It was clear to me from the outset that the further memoirs of the greatest hero in all France contains material of an inflammatory nature. For a start, René has written much of his diary for 1942 in a code which is so complex that at first I assumed I had scraped it off the ceiling in the wrong order.

René Fairfax
Artois Country
April 1989

1 JANUARY

Perhaps it is inevitable that, despite my continued attempts to turn the tides of war in our favour, my heroism remains unsung. My wife Edith offered to put things right at the party last night with a couple of verses detailing the exact nature of my achievements, but I modestly declined.

Only Yvette really appreciates the value of my work undercover. I sent a message to her yesterday morning: Meet me in the Gruber at eight o'nibble for a position. Lieutenant pantry was clocking his favourite Bols in at the bar again, and I only just escaped a drink.*

* *There is no question in my mind about the significance of this message. Though I have still not quite cracked René's code, those of us who are lucky enough to have been privy to his exploits will deduce that Nighthawk was about to strike once more for France.*

   During the course of such entries one begins to understand something of the complex nature of René's relationship with my mother, Yvette, though where 'the Gruber' fitted in one can only speculate.

Oh heck. Things are going very badly.

Ten months ago I was shot and apparently killed by a German firing squad. I have been in terrible pain ever since. Not only did the wooden bullets Colonel Von Strohm managed to substitute for the real ones leave appalling splinters, but also I have had to watch Edith inherit the café and spend all my money.

And that is not all.

I have had to expend a great deal of precious energy supervising Yvette and my new waitress, Mimi Labonq, as they serve under me.

I have had to expend even more backing away from the advances of Lieutenant Gruber, who is still suffering from the scars left by the Russian Front and will insist on trying to show them to me. Since my execution I have had to masquerade as René, my own twin brother from Nancy, and Hubert has never made a secret of his fondness for Nancy boys. Not recently, anyway.

The long and the short of it is that I was a shadow of my former self even before I was captured by Denise Laroque, my childhood sweetheart and now the fanatical leader of the Communist Resistance, in mid-December last year. I am a man who usually has no difficulty getting his Laroques off, but I have to say I was no match for Denise. She is insatiable. There were times when I thought it would be all over by Christmas.

Having offered myself for the freedom of my marginally less courageous comrades, I had no alternative but to lie back and think of England. Or Spain, or Sweden, or Switzerland – anywhere, in fact, where I could make a tactical withdrawal and live to fight another day.

After a week I was tempted to surrender. Fortunately, I was able to negotiate a settlement. I promised that we would be married when she had a moment to spare in-between blowing up trains and bridges and things, and as soon as I could take a break from my various acts of heroism.

In the meantime I agreed that she could borrow the original canvases of the Fallen Madonna with the Big Boobies by Van Clomp and the Cracked Vase with the Big Daisies by Van Gogh which I had cunningly concealed in the headquarters of the Communist Resistance. She said she would keep the forgeries I had as well.

3 JANUARY

I returned to downtown Nouvion a broken man. Fortunately Yvette was able to massage some feeling back into my aching limbs, and I was back in my usual position at the café in time to make the most of the season of goodwill. I'm glad to say the takings at the bar over the Christmas period were quite substantial as well.

I have only just recovered sufficient strength to begin recording my exploits once more for posterity.

René makes a small adjustment to his dickie. So does Monsieur Leclerc.

1·9·4·2

OPEN FOR BUSINESS

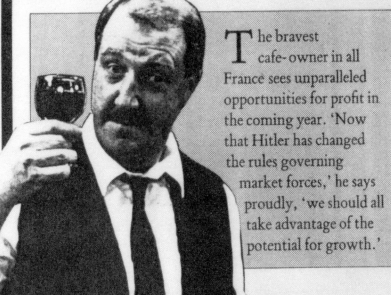

The bravest cafe-owner in all France sees unparalleled opportunities for profit in the coming year. 'Now that Hitler has changed the rules governing market forces,' he says proudly, 'we should all take advantage of the potential for growth.'

4 JANUARY

The New Year is traditionally a time for taking stock. As I polished the glasses at the bar this evening I ran through mine. It didn't take much time. Thanks to my wife's mother, we were short on gin. Thanks to Colonel Von Strohm and Captain Bertorelli we were long on knockwurst and salami. Thanks to Denise Laroque and the Nouvion West Sub Area of the Communist Resistance, we were short on canvases of the Fallen Madonna with the Big Boobies and the Cracked Vase with the Big Daisies.

'You are very preoccupied tonight, René,' Lieutenant Gruber said.

'You are going to have to get your lipstick and brushes out again, Lieutenant,' I replied.

'Ah, René.' He smiled that little smile of his that I find so unsettling. 'I have long dreamed of this moment. What do you have in mind?'

'Another couple of forgeries of the Fallen Madonna with the Big Boobies,' I said quickly.

5 JANUARY

My wife is still determined to marry me, despite her mother's advice and the threats of the fanatical leader of the Communist Resistance (Nouvion West Sub Area). As so often in life, this has its advantages and its disadvantages.

The disadvantages have been fairly obvious to anyone who has heard my wife sing. The advantage is that I got to spend an hour or so at the keyhole of the back room this afternoon watching Madame Lenare of the Brides Parisienne Boutique showing her some little items of lingerie for our wedding-night. And I must say they suited Madame Lenare very well.

For some reason, watching this exceptionally gifted woman in action reminded me forcibly of a particular painting by Van Clomp that I am anxious to get my hands on again. If I do not, General Von Klinkerhoffen will not get his forgery, nor will Herr Flick of the Gestapo and nor will Hitler who has already promised it to Eva for her birthday. Several times. Needless to say if they do not gain satisfaction they will each place a great deal of pressure on Colonel Von Strohm, who may in turn feel it necessary to mention my name.

It is fortunate in this instance that Lieutenant Gruber has artistic leanings. I decided to ask him if he was up to forging the Fallen Madonna with the Big Boobies from memory.

On second thoughts, I realised that this was one of my more optimistic schemes. He could have touched up the Laughing Cavalier with his eyes shut, but the Fallen Madonna required a slightly different approach.

Perhaps Madame Lenare could model for him. I checked the view through the key hole again and began to wonder whether we would ever be able to find enough paint.

6 JANUARY

Last night as we retired Edith approached me with the sort of twinkle in her eye that I am glad to say I have not encountered since the early days of our marriage.

'René,' she said, 'I have selected for our wedding-night some lovely surprises. Madame Lenare has some beautiful things under the counter.'

'She has some pretty good things above the counter,' I replied, wondering where all this would lead. I decided to take evasive action and suddenly remembered that I might have forgotten to turn the light off in the cellar.

As I descended the steps from the bar I had a brief, wistful memory of Maria before she posted herself to Switzerland in a Red Cross parcel. She used to get very dirty down there.

No sooner had the thought crossed my mind than a

pair of small but incredibly powerful arms encircled me and I felt Mimi Labonq's hot breath on the small of my back.

'Why are you trying to avoid me?' she whispered hoarsely. 'Now we are together let me do something that will make you feel warm and wonderful.'

'Good idea,' I said, attempting to shake her off. 'You can fill my hot-water bottle.'

I don't know what she does to the enemy, but she scares out of me the living daylights.

7 JANUARY

I've just found out what she does to the enemy, given half a chance.

Herr Flick of the Gestapo was entertaining Helga, the Colonel's personal secretary, in the back room tonight.

'Mimi,' I instructed, 'the menu, and wine for Herr Flick and his bit of . . . his lady.'

'I have already prepared a bottle for the Gestapo,' she growled.

I went swiftly through to check the table settings, and to make sure that the British airmen had already left by the window.

I was just closing the curtains when that idiot Crabtree appeared outside.

'Good moaning,' he said. His sense of time is only marginally better than his ability to speak our language.

'Good evening, officer. How comforting to know that you are doing your duty. Now go away and stop wasting your torch.'

'It is a dick night.'

'Very likely,' I said, my week with Denise flashing unaccountably before me.

'I thought I saw two men leaking by your dustbins.'

'Well that is France for you,' I said.

Mimi ushered Herr Flick into the room. 'Here you are, sir,' she growled. 'You will never drink a better bottle.'

Herr Flick about to knock up another Fallen Madonna.

'I will open it,' Herr Flick ordered.

'Herr Flick, when you behave in such a dominating fashion I go weak at the knees.' Helga's eyes shone.

'Only the knees?' I heard Flick reply as I left, pushing Mimi before me.

I felt it was time to give her a small lecture in the finer points of the restaurateur's art. I was tempted to give her a big lecture, but she simply wasn't the right height.

'Mimi,' I said authoritatively, 'you must not oversell our wine. We only give the Gestapo plonk, and it was very unwise telling him that he will never drink a better bottle.'

'It was the truth,' she growled. 'I removed the cork and put in the bottle a deadly poison. In four minutes he will be no more.'

'Mimi!' I cried, seeing my chances of a five-star rating in the *Michelin Guide* disappearing before my very eyes. 'Not in my café!'

I crashed through the door just as Herr Flick was giving the toast.

'May we be blessed with many little members of the Master Race . . .'

To his astonishment, I seized both glasses from their outstretched hands and emptied them on to the floor. The bottle I chucked out of the window.

There was a rather uneasy silence.

'It was not a good year,' I said.

20 JANUARY

For the last fortnight I have been quite unable to write. We men of action have to resign ourselves to the fact that moments of peaceful contemplation are often denied us. And what with avoiding the attentions of the Communist Resistance and attempting to prevent Mimi from wiping out a substantial proportion of my clientèle on the premises, I have been more or less perpetually on the move.

21 JANUARY

Last night I heard that Denise Laroque would still not rest until the women in my life have been rubbed out. The message was attached to a large stick of dynamite which came through the front window of the café, but fortunately extinguished itself in Lieutenant Gruber's port and lemon.

I wondered whether the moment had finally come for me to retire to the Spanish border and regroup.

I made a mental note of the defences that stood between me and the fanatical leader of the Communist Resistance as I poured the Lieutenant another drink.

There was Mimi, my little handgrenade, who was small but highly explosive at close quarters.

There was Yvette, my big bazooka, who was always prepared to deploy her weaponry on a variety of fronts.

And there was Edith, whom I have always looked upon as the ultimate deterrent.*

But what chance would they have if I stayed?

'You look troubled, René,' said Lieutenant Gruber.

'I'm just thinking about my arsenal,' I replied.

'Me too,' he said, with that little smile of his that I find so unsettling. 'Anything I can do to help?'

* *Edith Artois never gave up singing in public, even though she was asked to on many occasions. Even at the end of her life her vocal range was quite stunning.*

CAFÉ C·O·C·K

HUBERT TANKBANGER

Straight up with lily-of-the-valley and a hint of diesel. The only choice if you fancy a bender!

FALLEN MADONNA

If you fancy a hint of ripe melon, this is your idea of heaven. Fruity and spicey, full-bodied and irresistibly seductive. Large cups. Serves several. Beware of imitations!

FLYING HELMET

A house special! Decorated with wet celery, fruity, tart, beaten with an egg whisk, but be warned — this one's heavy on the wallet!

René t·a·i·l·s

APERITIF

What my wife's mother keeps in the glass by her bed. Heavy on the gin, strong on the nose.

HIMMLER SUNRISE

Lashings of tequila, a squeeze of orange, a pinch of salt, crushed ice and chopped nuts. Served with a twist!

RUSSIAN FRONT

An aquired taste, with plenty of ice.

PINK PANZER

Make tracks for B company's favourite snifter! Large Bols with a dash of pink. You'll be begging for another shot!

22 JANUARY

I was just reflecting earlier today that the old undertaker with the dicky ticker has not been sniffing around the café recently. Not since he sank a litre of embalming fluid by mistake on New Year's Eve and got thoroughly pickled.

I knew it was too good to last.

Yvette had just arranged a secret assignation* with me in the larder. We embraced, as heroes of the Resistance often do.

'Oh René,' she said, 'put around me your strong arms. Crush this yearning out of me. Put your rough cheek against mine. Run your rough hands through my hair. Press your rough lips to my lips. I would do anything for you.'

'Next time you go to the chemist, could you get for me a pot of skin cream?' I quipped.†

At that moment Monsieur Alfonse, the undertaker, entered the room.

'Monsieur!' he bellowed. 'What is this I see before me? The fiancé of the woman I love locked in the arms of another? Of a serving girl?'

'There is an explanation,' I said, thinking fast.

'To think that I have suppressed my desire for that adorable woman out of respect for your bravery and honour, and all the time you are doing a number behind her back! I shall go to her. And be warned, Monsieur, the gloves are off and I shall press my suit.'

'You will probably make a better job of it than she

---

* Assignment.

† There are a number of such exchanges throughout the diaries, and I can only assume that there is more to all this than meets the eye. My mother tells me that the clandestine nature of their meetings often led to some confusion, but that on this occasion she was ready for action and he, quite uncharacteristically, did not feel up to it.

would,' I said, attempting to lighten the atmosphere.

'I intend to tell her what I have seen,' he said, heading for the door.

'But Monsieur Alfonse,' I said reasonably, 'Frenchmen do not tell on other Frenchmen...'

'This is true,' he replied. 'But I have Belgian blood on my mother's side.'

Oh heck. Something tells me that the knockwurst is really going to hit the fan.

23 JANUARY

Lieutenant Gruber came in early yesterday evening. He was looking very frustrated. I hoped it didn't have anything to do with me.

'Your usual, Lieutenant?' I assumed he was there to enjoy a snifter.

'Ah René,' he replied, 'I ... Goodness, that is a very exciting perfume you are wearing.'

'In fact it is my aftershave,' I explained. 'It is a cologne for men.'

'No doubt that is why I am attracted to it. Can you bend over a little?'

Things looked as though they were about to get out of hand.

'I wish to speak with you confidentially,' the Lieutenant said. 'I am having a terrible time. It is the Italian.'

'The one whose picture is in your locket?'

'No, Bertorelli. Luckily the Colonel is sympathetic. He says the man does nothing but hang around the office and get in his hair.'

'But Lieutenant,' I said, 'the Colonel has very little hair.'

'Bertorelli is very persistent. And for me it is even worse. We share a billet.'

I raised my eyebrows. 'What does he get into of yours?'

'I'll have you know, René, that Captain Bertorelli will never be seen inside the uniform of an officer of the Tank Corps. And that goes particularly for B Company.'

'So where do I fit in?' I asked, wishing I hadn't.

'Colonel Von Strohm wants you to get the Resistance to blow him up.'

'That seems a little drastic.'

The Lieutenant nodded. 'Exactly what I said.'

'And?'

'Well, the Colonel decided that you should *almost* blow him up – you know, just enough to make him a nervous wreck so that he can be sent home.'

'My wife's singing might do the trick,' I suggested.

'Oh René, I knew I could count on you. I'll have his bags brought over to the café immediately.'

What-a mistake-a to make-a.

24 JANUARY

Bertorelli arrived just before breakfast. It is not going to be easy having him around. As Lieutenant Gruber warned me, he is an insufferable bore who spends the whole time boasting about his bravery and his conquests with women.*

If it wasn't for the fact that he is constantly wooing my wife Edith, I'd write him off as the sort of man who gives cowardice a bad name. I must console myself with the eight thousand francs he will be paying per night, and

---

* *This would have been especially offensive to a man for whom discretion was the better part of valour.*

the knowledge that Hubert can now concentrate on the forgeries in his chambers without fear of interruption.

We will of course risk his finding out about the radio in the bedroom of my wife's mother, but we heroes of the Resistance have learned to live with the constant fear of discovery. And besides, anyone who goes poking around in the bedroom of my wife's mother will get a lot more than he bargained for. I don't know how that old fool Leclerc keeps doing it.

25 JANUARY

I sent the increasingly ancient forger, Leclerc, out to replenish our dwindling stocks of gin this morning.

'How shall I disguise myself?' he asked.

'You will not need a disguise,' I said, exasperated. 'Go as yourself – as a perfectly normal idiot.'

In his absence I resolved to contact London and ask them when General de Gaulle, the tall one with the big hooter, would be sending my medals. While I was transmitting, Colonel Von Strohm and Lieutenant Gruber entered the café, and I thought I heard Captain Bertorelli coming up the stairs. As ever, I was able to keep my nerve. Wrenching the radio from its mountings in a single decisive movement, I hurled it out of the window. It landed on Leclerc, who was returning from his errand, but sadly it hit him on the head. As a result he is still absolutely all right.

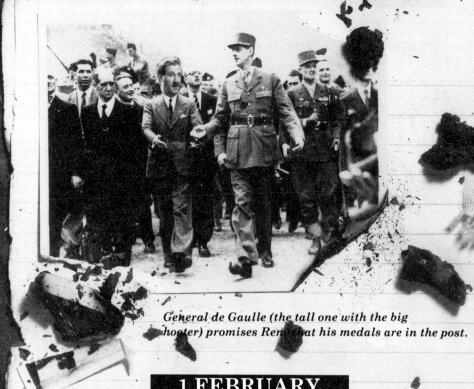

General de Gaulle (the tall one with the big hooter) promises Ren.. that his medals are in the post.

1 FEBRUARY

As I served him and the Colonel lunch, Bertorelli showed me the special gift that Mussolini wished him to confer upon General Von Klinkerhoffen.

'It is the Italian War Hero Medal,' he beamed.

'I don't believe I've ever seen one before,' I said.

'I think they are very rare,' the Colonel said.

Talking about medals reminds me. Mine have still not arrived. However, Michelle of the Resistance appeared in the back room as Yvette and I were deciding upon the evening's menu. Michelle is still completely obsessed with me, so I felt I had to offer her a nibble. She told me that she had already eaten.

'Then what are you doing here in broad daylight?' I asked.

'Listen very carefully,' she said. 'I shall say this only once. A new radio has arrived for you. It will be delivered by a man disguised as a mountaineer.'

'But the nearest mountain is one hundred miles away,' I pointed out patiently.

'He is lost,' she said. 'Naturally he will come in here for directions.'

'Naturally,' I said.

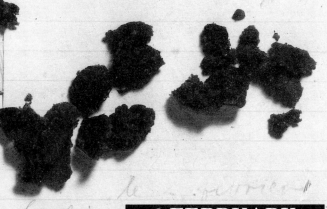

2 FEBRUARY

Lieutenant Gruber came into the bar at about nine. I asked Mimi to pour him his usual, and reminded her of my little house rule about not killing people on the premises. I also reminded her of the Lieutenant's artistic leanings, and the fact that many of those leanings were in my direction.

'Who is to blame him?' she whispered hoarsely. 'You have a quality that is irresistible. From the moment I saw you my lips hungered for your lips.'

'Here,' I said, rather hurriedly handing her a slice of ripe brie. 'Practise on this. I am rather busy.'

'Will you join me for a little snifter, René?' Hubert said.

'I've only got time for a drink, I'm afraid,' I replied. 'How are you getting on with the paintings?'

'I am forging ahead, René, but it is quite a task. The Fallen Madonna is very demanding.'

'Yes,' I said. 'You can see it in her smile.'

'And in her ...'

'Yes,' I agreed. 'Those too.'

Nouvion 1941
A year of ups and downs.

My agent called to offer me another big part.

Hope I'm in the running.

I'm gonna wash that man right out of mein Herr.

I did it my way.

Here's goggling at you, kid.

3 FEBRUARY

The Colonel was waiting outside the café as I opened for business.

'I have arranged to meet my assistant here, René. I just wanted to remind you that he knows nothing of the British airmen, or the paintings, or the cuckoo clock.'

'I had forgotten about the cuckoo clock,' I said.

'Nor does he know about my ventures upstairs with the girls,' he continued, with a nod towards Yvette.

'With the flying helmet and the wet celery?' she asked.

'Do not mention the flying helmet and the wet celery.'

I nodded. 'Rely on us Colonel. But wouldn't life be a lot simpler if you just sent him back to Italy?'

'Undoubtedly,' he sighed. 'But Hitler still insists that an Itie unit will be coming with us when we invade England.'

'When is the invasion?' Yvette asked. 'I thought it had been cancelled.'

The Colonel looked flustered. 'Invasion? I should never have told you. Forget it.'

'Yes,' I said. 'Forget it, Yvette. Never mention the invasion or the fact that the Colonel told you about it. By the way, Colonel, we are running out of butter and sugar and paraffin and cigarettes.'

Captain Bertorelli arrived as the Colonel was taking down quantities.

'Colonnello! You my friend and I keep-a you waiting. But you forgive-a me, no?' He kissed the Colonel on both cheeks.

'Patron!' He kissed me on both cheeks.

'Pretty lady!' He kissed Yvette on both cheeks.

'Lieutenant!' He shook Gruber's hand.

At that moment I caught sight of the old forger Leclerc trying to come through the front door. With a rucksack, fifty metres of rope and an ice-pick to carry, it wasn't easy.

'Good evening,' he croaked. 'Can anybody help an old mountaineer who has lost his way?'

'Oh my God. Come here old mountaineer and tell me your problem.' My problem was that I should have thrown *him* out of the window instead of the radio.

'It is I, Leclerc.'

I suggested that this was abundantly clear to all but the totally blind.

'In the pack on my back is a new radio. It is already connected up to the batteries, and this ice-pick is the aerial.'

At that moment the rucksack started to play 'Somebody Stole My Girl' and then produced a series of static emissions of which even my wife's mother would have been proud.

Since the silly old fool was too exhausted to climb the stairs I had to sit him next to Bertorelli, hand him a bowl of soup and hope for the best.

The emissions continued.

Bertorelli, not knowing quite how to react, complimented Leclerc on the quality of his coat.

'It is a windcheater,' the bogus mountaineer corrected him.

The Itie spoke for them all: 'Whatever you do don't-a take it off-a.'

4 FEBRUARY

Yvette and I took the opportunity of spending an hour or so together in the back room this afternoon. I thought it was high time we got familiar

with the new   book

all sorts of different things to learn.*

Our session was interrupted by Michelle of the Resistance.

'Listen carefully,' she said, 'I shall say this only once.'

'What?' I asked.

'I shall say this only once,' she repeated.

'No,' I said. 'What will you say?'

'We have found a way of discovering what goes on in the dungeon of Herr Flick of the Gestapo.'

'But Michelle,' I said, 'there are some things even a Frenchman does not want to know.'

* *Fragments of this conversation will remain forever shrouded by Christmas pudding. It is quite clear, however, that René and my mother were examining the new code book very closely, each absolutely determined to crack it.*

'We have information that the Gestapo are now convinced there is a plot to blow up Hitler.'

Well, that would mean one less forgery of the Fallen Madonna with the Big Boobies for Hubert Gruber to worry about. 'Have you placed within the dungeon a listening device?'

'It was not necessary. Von Smallhausen forgot his keys yesterday and blew the door off with some Gestapo dynamite. As a result it is possible to hear everything Herr Flick says from down the corridor.'

The bravest café-owner in all France explains to a disappointed Hitler that the Fallen Madonna with the Big Boobies must remain in French hands.

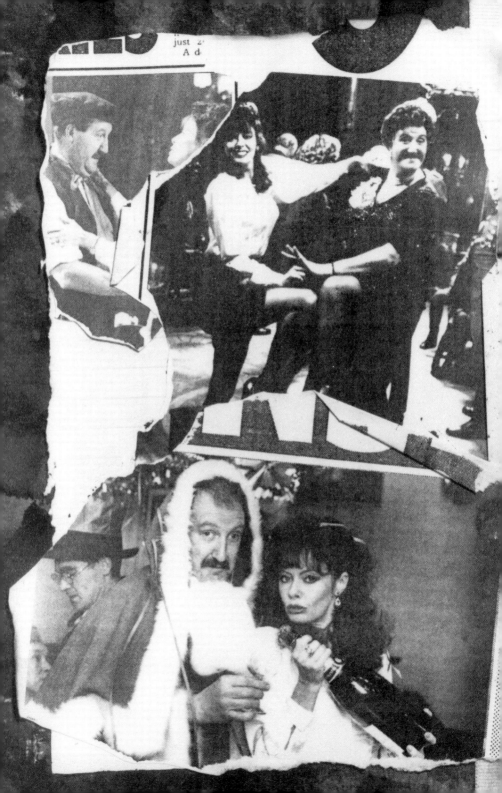

Shortly after the war René Artois filled the office of Mayor of Nouvion.
My mother says this surprised nobody; it was a very small office. During
his first term, however, there was a scandalous attempt to undermine
his reputation by implications in the local press that Yvette, who had
been taken on as a Town Hall researcher, had had 'relations' with a
string of powerful and not always salubrious men.

Fortunately, René was able to put an end to these ludicrous rumours by
explaining that Yvette was a professional, and had been working
undercover at the time.

I was just finishing off my boiled egg and soldiers in the back room this morning when I heard the old undertaker with the dicky ticker apologise to Yvette in the bar for his behaviour the other day.

'I am so consumed with jealousy,' he said, 'I am forgetting how we Frenchmen have this great tradition of having it off like rabbits.'

I listened more closely, wondering if his change of tone meant that I was off the hook. Just then, Edith came down the stairs. I held my breath.

'Dear lady,' he began, 'I think of you day and night. Even when I am embalming, it is your face that haunts me through the fluid.'

I knew the feeling. The same thing happens to me when I am boiling up goat's head soup.

'I can no longer contain my passion. I must kiss those tempting, sensuous lips.'

'Oh Monsieur Alfonse,' came the reply. 'You are very naughty. But, as you put it so nicely, you can have one little peck.'

There was a gasp, followed by a muffled thud as the undertaker's ticker failed to take the strain and he hit the floor. If my wife's lips are capable of putting such a burden on a man's big muscle, I reflected, it was just as well she had withheld the rest of her. I suddenly began to see Madame Lenare's creations for our wedding-night in a rather different light.

11 FEBRUARY

We had spent the best part of the day – the part I usually like to spend in my private quarters with Yvette pressing my aprons* – attempting to revive my rival and clear the café for the evening's business. Sometimes I wish he would just go and bury himself.

As soon as Monsieur Alfonse had consumed enough of my best cognac to fuel his return home, Helga appeared. I knew it was Helga because she was dressed in Herr Flick's sinister leather coat and hat, and very little else.

Despite her engagement to Herr Flick, and a slightly excessive appetite for long periods of interrogation, Helga is good news, particularly when she is out of uniform. This seems to happen increasingly often.

'Don't tell me,' I said, 'Herr Flick has once again walked off in your clothes. He is even now trying to eavesdrop on General Von Klinkerhoffen, disguised as Irma Von Kinkenrotten, a temporary female stenographer of the opposite sex.'

Helga shook her head. 'The last time he tried that the General had him arrested and thrown in the klink. He is of the opinion that the General thinks I am a nice bit of crackling, so this time he is masquerading as my not-quite-identical twin sister from Heidelberg. He suspects that the General and the Colonel are closely involved in a plot to blow up Hitler.'

'I don't wish to know any of this,' I said cunningly.

'But René,' she said, 'don't you see? If the Colonel is

---

* *It seems extraordinary that the bravest café-owner in all France would personally supervise such a mundane task, but my mother assures me that much of what they did together was ten per cent inspiration, ninety per cent perspiration.*

tortured the Gestapo might discover that the closest anyone is going to get to the Fallen Madonna with the Big Boobies is a forgery by Lieutenant Gruber, painted from memory. And it won't stop there ...'

'It never does,' I said, making a mental note to re-acquaint myself with the quickest route to the Spanish border.

13 FEBRUARY

Things have gone very quiet, I was thinking to myself this morning. Too quiet. Perhaps I should just turn my back on the life of heroism and excitement I had carved for myself in Nouvion and give someone else a go.

No sooner was I reaching for my suitcase and route map than there was a great commotion in the courtyard and Lieutenant Gruber appeared. All of a sudden, turning my back didn't seem to be a terribly good idea. Especially as his face was suffused with pleasure and a fine sheen of perspiration glistened on his upper lip.

My first thought was that he had arrived to give me my Valentine's card a day early. In fact, he had just been exercising one of the General's horses, a magnificent black stallion.

'René, there is nothing like the sight of a handsome beast with nostrils flaring, foam flying from the mouth, clattering over the cobbles scattering peasants.'

'Yes,' I said, 'I expect the horse enjoyed it too. You had better sit down, Lieutenant.'

Over a cognac, he revealed to me the true reason for his visit.

'Something rather extraordinary has happened, René.'

'I'm getting used to it,' I said.

'General Von Klinkerhoffen has placed in custody Herr Flick of the Gestapo who has been spying on him whilst in the disguise of Helga's nearly-identical twin sister from Heidelberg.'

'I don't imagine that Himmler's reaction will look too good on the General's CV.'

'He has thought of that. Herr Flick has been arrested on suspicion of being Irma Von Kinkenrotten, a temporary female secretary of the opposite sex who escaped his grasp once before.'

'It all seems fairly straightforward,' I said.

Just a little puff in the bath.

14 FEBRUARY

I have learnt to approach this particular Saint's Day with some caution, especially since Hubert Gruber returned from the Russian Front and Edith started going to night classes with Madame Lenare.

Mimi decided to celebrate by inviting Captain Bertorelli up to her room and tearing him limb from limb.

She remained technically within the limits of my little house rule, but the Itie was in bad shape when he came down for lunch.

Yvette decided to celebrate by taking me into the larder and showing me a Valentine's message that she had tattooed on to her left ▓▓▓▓▓ because she hadn't been able to find a card. Unfortunately I had left my reading glasses upstairs, so I had to get really close and then we

absolutely covered in Brie.*

Edith was sent a rather dog-eared heart with a big question mark on it.

'It is from a secret admirer,' she beamed.

I couldn't help feeling that it might have been from someone quite old with a dicky ticker.

Apart from that, however, very little has happened. I think I'll stop here and have an early night.

---

* *René often reminds us that certain things were in short supply during these dark days, even for a hero of the Resistance. Taking this into account, it still seems remarkably inventive of my mother to tattoo her message on some leftover Brie.*

15 FEBRUARY

I spoke too soon.

Just as I was about to get into my pyjamas Lieutenant Gruber roared up to the café and shouted my name. I leaned out of the upstairs window and told him that I was very touched, but a card would have been sufficient.

'Not on this occasion, René,' he called. 'I have urgent need of you in my little tank.'

I didn't ask him to elaborate, not within earshot of the neighbours anyway. As soon as I got downstairs he told me proudly that he had completed the forgeries, and that they were really very beautiful, considering that they were of a woman and a cracked vase.

I told him that I was delighted, but that sadly a prior engagement prevented me from returning with him to his chambers to admire his handiwork.

I think he was a little disappointed, but I had a nagging feeling that where boobies are concerned, there's no substitute for the real thing. And the real thing was still in the Nouvion West Sub Area headquarters of the Communist Resistance.

I cannot say that I have missed Herr Flick's regular presence in the back room, because the Gestapo never pays its bills. Also, I have to admit, it's nice to see Helga on her own from time to time, particularly since she has not yet got all her clothes back.

I sat at her table for a moment or two and asked her how her fiancé was getting on. She told me that only that overgrown fruit-bat Von Smallhausen had been allowed in to see him.

'That must really have cheered him up,' I said.

'Yes,' said Helga. 'Herr Flick has always appreciated Von Smallhausen's sense of humour. He offered Herr Flick a suicide pill to crush between his teeth so no one would know what a fool he had made of himself.'

'I bet that went down well.'

'Herr Flick told him he was very, very stupid. Von Smallhausen replied that he, on the other hand, was not chained up in a dungeon wearing women's clothing.'

'Something tells me that it won't be long before Himmler hears of this.'

'Herr Flick has ordered Von Smallhausen to get a message to Berlin to explain his predicament.'

'It's going to take a bit of explaining,' I said.

23 FEBRUARY

It may be that Herr Flick's incarceration had something to do with the festive mood in the café this evening. The only false note was provided by Edith, who insisted on testing the mettle of her audience by singing 'It's a Long Way to Tipperary.'

'It's a long, long way to Tipperary,' she concluded after what seemed like hours, 'but my heart's right there.'

'What a pity the rest of her isn't,' the Colonel said.

As everyone gradually summoned up the courage to remove the cheese from their ears, conversation resumed.

'Come and sit with us, René,' Lieutenant Gruber entreated. 'I have brought with me the completed forgeries of the paintings.'

He placed a number of knockwurst sausages proudly on the table. They were joined more or less immediately by four or five more, deposited with his usual ceremony by the Itie, Bertorelli.

'Look-a what my mama send for us from Italy. The black-a de market salami. Take-a de sniff – is beautiful, no?'

Apparently Bertorelli's sausages were destined to be a gift for Edith as soon as the gallant Captain had been for a cut-a de hair. I hoped they might keep her off my back for a while.

No sooner had he left than that idiot Crabtree arrived with a consignment of dynamite that Michelle wanted me to store in the cellar. Honestly, that girl will go to any lengths to provide herself with an excuse to have regular liaisons with me.

Crabtree had obviously spent some time deciding upon the most original way of transporting the explosives without arousing suspicion.

'Good moaning,' he said, as he eased his way delicately towards the bar. 'The deenamote is inside the sisages.'

'Thank you, Officer, you could not have come at a better time,' I said, showing him the door.

I had hardly had time to count the sausages when Mimi alerted us to the fact that General Von Klinkerhoffen was heading in our direction. Luckily we were able to hide every single one down the front of Lieutenant Gruber's trousers and Helga's bosom. The evening was full of surprises.

25 FEBRUARY

I had always known that tampering with the front of Lieutenant Gruber's trousers would have drastic repercussions, but I was not prepared to be dragged from my bed early yesterday morning and frogmarched to the German Headquarters.

When I was hurled through the door of the Colonel's office I saw that both Helga and Lieutenant Gruber were with him. One look at their faces told me that they were under a lot of pressure from General Von Klinkerhoffen. That usually meant one of two things. Either we would all test out the effectiveness of the escape route to Switzerland, or I would be shot. And since I did not have the original canvas of The Fallen Madonna with the Big Boobies to bargain with, it looked like Goodnight Nouvion.

'René,' Lieutenant Gruber said fiercely, 'we are very cross with you.'

'Yes, René,' the Colonel spat. 'You have a lot of explaining to do. We have examined the sausages and it is clear to us that you are working for the Resistance again.'

'The two concealed down my bosom were dynamite,' Helga said, somewhat unnecessarily.

'And supposing I'd got something hot down the front of my trousers?' Lieutenant Gruber asked.

I looked from one to another. 'There is no answer to that.'

'The dynamite would have exploded – and I have not even made a will!'

'You would have died intestate,' I said.

There was an uneasy silence.

'I think we should forget all this nonsense about me being the bravest Resistance Leader in all France,' I bluffed, 'and spend a bit of time sorting out which knockwurst is which.'

'I agree, René,' said Hubert. 'Perhaps you could give me a hand with these . . .'

Thankfully we had the whole lot lined up on the Colonel's desk without too much fuss.

Lieutenant Gruber put an end to the confusion: 'Those are the forgeries of The Cracked Vase with the Big Daisies by Van Gogh which are to go to the General, one of which he will send to Hitler believing it is a forgery, and one of which he will keep himself believing it is a genuine Van Gogh, but which of course is a forgery. Those others are the forgeries of The Fallen Madonna with the Big Boobies by Van Clomp which were to go to Herr Flick, of which he would have sent one to Hitler, and the other he would have kept himself believing it to be the original which he will sell after the war, but which of course is also a forgery, and anyway he does not need either at the moment.'

'Why is this?' I asked.

'Because Herr Flick is in the nick,' the Colonel said.

'What for?' I asked innocently.

'For spying on me and the General, wearing Helga's clothes.'

I wanted to ask what he and the General were doing in Helga's clothes, but on this occasion discretion was the better part of valour.

I made my way back to the inevitable hero's welcome at the café. Since the Colonel wanted the forgeries returned to their hiding place in my cellar, I had a great many knockwurst down the front of my trousers. Something in Yvette's and Mimi's expressions told me that they could see how pleased I was to be back with them.

Always a great respecter of tradition, it appears that René was planning on reviving the coat-of-arms of the Barons Artois of Nouvion, to whom he claimed to be directly related.

Experts will note the imaginative employment of a number of arcane heraldic devices, including the three knockwursts rampant and the wet celery dormant.

11 MARCH

Despite appearances, I was not ready to get immediately back into action. I wasn't in the mood for writing much either.

So another fortnight has passed. I thought occasionally of Herr Flick, chained spread-eagled in the château dungeon, especially when Mimi pinned me down in the cellar and demanded a rise. That girl is very trying. It is no time at all since she replaced Maria, and already she is impossible to satisfy. I spent some time explaining how difficult things are for me at the moment and then just had to put my foot down and tell her she couldn't have one.

Apart from anything else, how would Yvette feel?

12 MARCH

Helga has been thinking of Herr Flick too. Apart from anything else, he is still dressed in her underwear.

She had five minutes with him this afternoon.

'Was that enough?' I asked.

'Not at all,' she replied wistfully. 'He is in such an unusual position. It is very painful for him. But it is also instructive. I think he is taking notes.'

'Could you do nothing for him?'

'I asked him how I could relieve his situation. He told me he could not endure the agony in his legs and demanded a pair of scissors.'

'It would take a while for him to cut through his chains

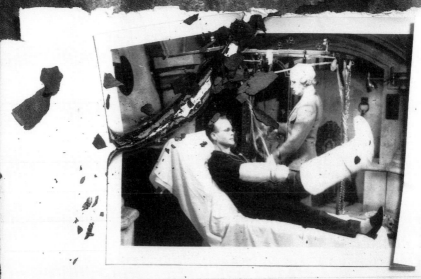

Herr Flick attempts to get his leg over.

with those,' I said, as one who has often thought of trying
nonetheless.

She shook her head.

'He wanted to cut through his tight knicker elastic.'

At that instant four of my best glasses shattered
behind the bar. I thought Denise and her friends were
paying us another visit, but no such luck. Edith had started
singing.

'Always have ready a dustpan and brush at times like
this,' I chided Mimi.

Yvette signalled me to move through for a secret
meeting in the back room.

'Who wants me?' I asked as I shut the door.

'I do,' she said.

I've got to hand it to Yvette. There was a time when
Michelle was taking much of the initiative in our
undercover work, but these days the balls are definitely
back in Yvette's court.

'Do you not ache for some action at such moments as
this?' she whispered.

'I am occasionally a bit stiff,' I replied, 'but I put it
down to age.'

15 MARCH

Needless to say, it wasn't long before we saw the sort of action Yvette yearned for.

Last night Michelle of the Resistance tapped like a phantom on the window of the back room. Monsieur Alfonse was with her.

'I brought this intrepid lady here in the back of my small hearse with the small horse,' he explained.*

'Monsieur,' I said, 'if she is discovered you could be shot.'

'I know, but it is worth it.'

'He does this for France,' Michelle said.

'And three hundred francs a mile plus waiting time,' Monsieur Alfonse reminded her.

'I will pay him only once,' Michelle said.

She was there to warn us that Himmler is not pleased about Herr Flick's disappearance, and we can all expect a big stink. The General has wind of this, and has ordered the Colonel and the Lieutenant to disguise themselves as members of the Resistance and help Herr Flick escape. They will then lead him into an ambush.

* *Monsieur Alfonse left the small hearse with the small horse to Edith in his will. She used it to do the shopping.*

16 MARCH

'There is only one problem, René,' the Colonel said as he gave me their version. 'To ensure that we are not shot along with Herr Flick we have to wear a small cornflower in our hats.'

'I think that sunflowers would give us a better chance,' the Lieutenant said.

I'd be tempted to take along an entire bush.

19 MARCH

I've had a very nasty feeling about Herr Flick's position for some time. I now know why.

I was foolish enough to be attracted by Helga as she sat by the fountain this afternoon. I can't quite get used to the fact that she is still missing many of her clothes.

'Sit here,' she said, pointing beside her.

'I do not wish to be seen in the square fraternising,' I said.

'How would you like to be seen dead?' she asked.

I shrugged. Girls had chatted me up like this many times before. I always gave the same answer.

'I will fraternise.'

'Herr Flick is close to cracking. If he does so he may spill the beans about the forgeries of the Fallen Madonna with the ...'

'Dynamite bosom?' I suggested, eyeing what lay behind Herr Flick's sinister leather lapels.

She nodded. 'Gruber will be next. He will implicate us, the trail will lead to you and you will be shot.'

'Thank you for warning me. I will leave at once for the Spanish border on that idiot policeman's bicycle.'

'You would not get ten yards,' she said.

'Why not?'

'Because I can shoot ten yards.'

'How can I help?' I asked.

29 MARCH

I shouldn't have asked.

Before you could say 'sinister leather overcoat' I was on my way to the château with Helga and Von Smallhausen to rescue Herr Flick. My moustache was newly trimmed, my glasses newly appropriated from my wife's mother.

You've guessed it. Even though I am shorter than Himmler, fatter than Himmler, younger than Himmler, balder than Himmler and cannot speak German, I was masquerading as Heinrich Himmler.

Worse was to come.

René Artois' Nouvion *was the greatest bestseller in all France in the late 1940s. The map which follows was folded into the Christmas pudding, and appears to be an early draft of a feature he intended to include. My mother tells me it depicts some of René's favourite walks.*

I was in the back of the sinister Gestapo staff car with Von Smallhausen. Helga drove.

'What do I do if anyone speaks to me?' I asked.

'Hit them with your whip,' she said.

I was just thinking of practising on Von Smallhausen when a bullet richocheted past my newly trimmed moustache. I must admit I was unnerved. We heroes of the Resistance are often shot at, but only occasionally by our own side.

As a result, I was almost glad when we arrived at the General's Headquarters and I was able to calm myself by whipping a few guards who were impertinent enough to greet me. But not for long. As soon as we entered Herr Flick's cell, the rescue plan took a sinister turn. Herr Flick ordered Von Smallhausen to hand over his gun and used it to persuade me to take off my clothes. Helga told me that when he was in that sort of mood it was better to strip first and ask questions later.

Suffice it to say that not long afterwards Herr Flick had made good his escape disguised as Heinrich Himmler, leaving me chained to a pillar in Helga's underwear. Sadly, there was no room in them for Helga as well.

31 MARCH

The Colonel and the Lieutenant arrived moments later, disguised as Gestapo. They both wore sinister leather coats and hats, but surprisingly it was Von Strohm who had the limp.

'René,' the Lieutenant greeted me. 'You are the last person we expected to see, especially dressed like that – not that it doesn't suit you.'

'I have been double-crossed,' I said.

'I can see that,' Hubert replied. 'And your stockings are wrinkled.'

1 APRIL

This is no joke. The memory of those hours as a prisoner still returns to haunt me as I write. I find I simply cannot keep it up. Yvette, particularly, is generous with her support,* but only time will tell whether I can fully recover.

---

* *I myself have often had reason to be grateful for this sort of support from my editor.*

2 APRIL

Lieutenant Gruber returned much later with the keys to my wrist irons. As he released me he expressed his hope that I would soon be able to remove the experience from my memory.

I hope he will have more success than I have had.

3 APRIL

I suppose I can't complain. At least I've had no trouble from the idiot British airmen recently. They've spent almost two months living in the dustbins outside the windows of the back room.

I must say I wouldn't fancy living off the stale bread and mouldy potato peel that Leclerc covers them with from time to time, but they don't seem to mind. They pop out occasionally to use the pissoir, but only to post letters.

Monsieur Alfonse, on the other hand, is still getting right up my nose, and it's not just the embalming fluid. I

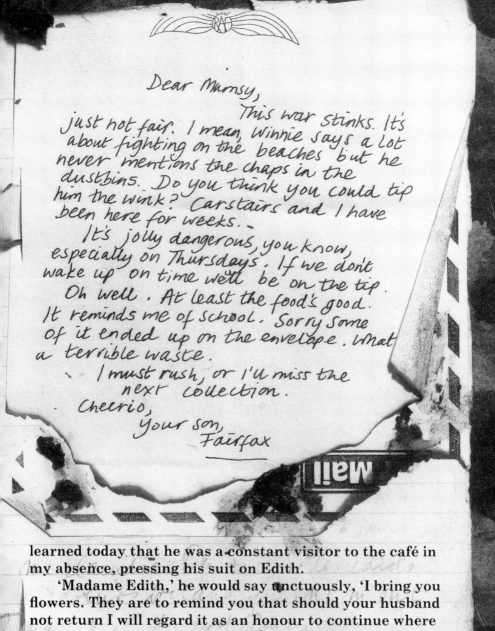

Dear Mumsy,

This war stinks. It's just not fair. I mean, Winnie says a lot about fighting on the beaches but he never mentions the chaps in the dustbins. Do you think you could tip him the wink? Carstairs and I have been here for weeks.

It's jolly dangerous, you know, especially on Thursdays. If we don't wake up on time we'll be on the tip.

Oh well. At least the food's good. It reminds me of school. Sorry some of it ended up on the envelope. What a terrible waste.

I must rush, or I'll miss the next collection.

Cheerio,
Your son,
Fairfax

learned today that he was a constant visitor to the café in my absence, pressing his suit on Edith.

'Madame Edith,' he would say unctuously, 'I bring you flowers. They are to remind you that should your husband not return I will regard it as an honour to continue where he left off.'

If that is the case, he has a lot of catching up to do. I left off before Hitler was halfway down the Polish Corridor.

10 APRIL

That idiot Crabtree assures me that I should be grateful that the RAF are still farting for freedom, and in a way I am.

As I selflessly attempted with my torch to direct their bombs away from my loved ones and towards the café-owner with a bigger one across the square, I came upon Yvette trembling in a doorway.

'Big bangs frighten me,' she said.

'It is only natural,' I replied.

We were almost immediately interrupted by Edith, who has been known to put even a squadron of Wellingtons to flight. I don't know how many times I've had to explain how Yvette's duty at a time like this is to shield the body of the bravest man in all France from rogue shrapnel, but tonight makes one more.

11 APRIL

As dawn broke, I realised that last night's air-raid has left us with bad news and good news.

The bad news is that the café-owner across the square is still very much in business. The good news is that we seem to have got rid of the British airmen.

12 APRIL

It is too much to hope that their own side dropped a very large bomb on them, but I'm keeping my fingers crossed.

13 APRIL

It was too much.

However, they are out of my hair. They've given themselves up to the local policeman, who is himself a British agent in disguise, and should therefore have the responsibility of organising their return to England.

14 APRIL

They're back in my hair.

Crabtree has released them on the grounds of insufficient evidence.

15 APRIL

And if that's not enough, I've got to put my head back in the den of Denise Laroque, the fanatical ex-lion tamer, in order to repossess the original canvases of the Fallen Madonna with the Big Boobies and the Cracked Vase with the Big Daisies.

I have to do this because Herr Flick wants them, because the General wants them, because the Colonel wants them, and because Hitler still wants to give one to Eva for her birthday. And because if I don't I will be shot.

Since discovering that Denise is due to go to a Communist Resistance fund-raising dinner in Brest in a week's time, I have also experienced a revival in my ambition to see the Fallen Madonna safely into French hands.

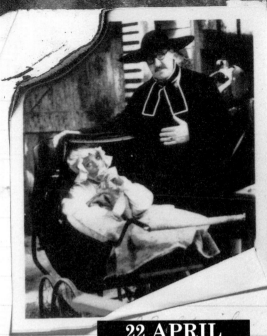

22 APRIL

It is possible that one or two people were a little surprised to see the bravest café-owner in all France dressed as a Roman Catholic vicar wheeling a pram through the countryside. Poor Yvette, I know, was positively beside herself. I think she probably knows that vicars only have very small stipends, and was worried about how long I would be able to keep it up.

   Why exactly *was* I dressed as a Roman Catholic vicar wheeling a pram with Mimi Labonq inside it dressed as a baby? It is a good question, and the answer is simple. Mimi's nappy was covering something that is very special and dear to me, an object of beauty that I am hoping will bring much joy and comfort to a retired café-owner in his old age. I could hardly wait to get her home and run my hands over it again.*

---

* *Rene refers, of course, to the painting of the Fallen Madonna with the*
  Big Boobies by Van Clomp. Somehow the Cracked Vase with the Big
  Daisies by Van Gogh never held the same allure for him.

23 APRIL

I didn't get home.

It is the early hours of the morning and there is no one in the deserted sawmill but me and my alarmingly devoted serving girl. Is there time, I wonder, for a quick entry?

I think I'll chance it. The Colonel and the Itie with the dead chicken on his head were supposed to create a diversion so that I could make off with the paintings. But, knowing them, they have probably been ambushed by the Communist Resistance and captured, and even at this moment are being brought here at gunpoint by Denise Laroque, the fanatical head of the Communist Resistance (Nouvion West Sub Area) who is as madly in love with me as ever.

Ah ...*

---

* *Always ready for action, René had brought his diary with him – disguised, perhaps, as a Bible. But after all the excitement, there does not seem to have been enough lead left in his pencil for what he had in mind.*

I was right.

Lieutenant Gruber, Colonel Von Strohm, Leclerc and the odious Itie were bundled into the room before I'd even finished my sentence.

It didn't looked good for any of us, but luckily it looked absolutely terrible for Leclerc in particular. The girls from the Communist Resistance suspected him of leading the Germans to their secret hideout. They told him they wanted to take him outside and put him up against a wall.

The silly old fool thought he'd got lucky. Then the truth dawned on him.

'He made me do it,' he blustered, pointing at the Colonel. 'I would die for France.'

'Then why didn't you?' Denise asked reasonably.

Leclerc paused.

'I will eventually ...'

As a man of the cloth it was clearly up to me to intercede on behalf of the frail old piano-tuning peasant. But how could I best persuade them to spare his life? I decided to tell them the truth.

'He has the mind of a five-year-old,' I said. 'He has a condition known in the medical world as "gaga".'

What happened next surprised us all. Captain Bertorelli, despite being Italian, and an Italian in the Italian army to boot, stepped boldly forward to face the guns. Perhaps he mistook them for ice-cream cones. I've suspected his eyesight since he first called my wife beautiful.

'Why you so damned aggressive, eh?' he asked. 'You should not make-a the war, you should make-a the love.'

'Does anyone fancy this Italian before we shoot him?' Denise asked.

'He could be quite amusing for an hour or two,' said a girl whose body had up until then been hidden by one of the barn doors, but only just.

'I want-a to make-a the last request,' said Bertorelli.

'I must have-a the blindfold.'

'Before you are shot?' Denise asked.

'No. Before I make-a the love ...'

It was time for someone brave and fearless to take charge and suggest that we could get for the Germans a large ransom.

'We are all good Communists,' I said masterfully. 'Let us form a committee and have a debate and put a motion on the table. You need party funds – you could start a newspaper and advertise for members.'

Denise agreed with me. Girls often do. They find my ideas penetrating.

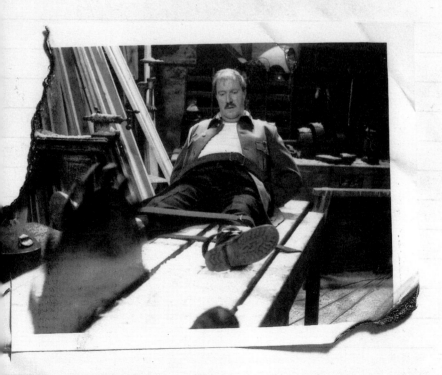

René Artois, seconds away from becoming two of the bravest men in all France.

21 MAY

I have often heard Herr Flick say how good Helga is down
in his dungeon for a bit of

other,

screwing   slap and tickle

Favourite

explosive   how   your father?*
He also spends a lot of time watching other people in
action. Apparently he had had me under strict

* *Another passage that has been rendered obscure by Christmas*
  pudding. Nonetheless I have used my increasingly detailed
  knowledge of the participants to piece together the missing portions
  of text as follows:
  'dungeon for a bit of interrogation about some misdemeanour or other.
  The interrogation might entail some thumb-screwing, and failure to
  answer the questions would result in the use of the old slap and tickle
  technique. Favourite questions to Resistance members would include:
  Where does your mother keep the explosives, and how about your
  father?'

surveillance as I wheeled Mimi's pram towards the sawmill. Helga was dressed as a nursemaid and Herr Flick as a baby in a pram. He wore a sinister black leather bonnet, and a nappy with little blue swastikas on it.

'Can you see anything through your powerful Gestapo binoculars, Herr Flick?' Helga asked him.

'The Colonel, the Lieutenant and the Italian Captain are surrounded by rough working-class women with guns. We must assume that their plans have failed.'

'What do we do now?'

'Wheel me back to my headquarters – and do not go over any bumps as I wish to go to the potty.'

Herr Flick's knob is so big...

...that he sometimes needs to keep it in a sling.

The idiot policeman gave Edith and Yvette the massage
that I had been kiptured by the Kimmunist Resostance.

'No!' Yvette screamed, grasping at once the enormity
of my ~~pr~~dic *

Crabtree pulled out a small bottle from beneath his
cape.

'Put these smelling silts under your neese and have a
good sniff.'

But Yvette need not have worried. I have trained
Michelle well. My protegée announced that she had a
brilliant plan.

* *Predicament.*

23 MAY

Brilliant. She only wanted to call in the RAF from London and have their bombers drop bombs on a sawmill not a million kilometres from where I was standing.

She said the hated Germans and the Communists were together under one roof, and I would be proud to die for France. And so I shall – in good time. Meanwhile I fully intend to live for France. Heroes of the Resistance are in short supply in the Nouvion area, so my particular qualities of leadership and courage are rarely seen.

Monsieur Alfonse took a different view.

'He will die a happy man,' the eager embalmer said to Edith, 'knowing that I will marry you, dear lady, and look after you tenderly for the few years remaining to me before leaving to you the very large quantity of money in my Swiss bank account – the number of which I will reveal just before we blow out the candle on the night of our honeymoon.'

24 MAY

The girls at last agreed that I should be allowed to go and try to get a ransom for the prisoners. One million francs for the Germans seems to be the going rate, and ten tins of baked beans for the Itie. That sounded fair – especially as baked beans are on special offer at the butcher with the big chopper.

Before I set off on my dangerous mission, the Colonel made me retrieve the paintings from their hiding place behind the beam. Little did he realise they were forgeries; the real ones, by this time, were warm and snug in the nappy of Mimi Labonq. But I was happy to humour him.

'Put them down Gruber's trousers,' the Colonel said.

I hesitated.

'Would you like them on the left or the right, Lieutenant?' I asked.

'I think, if it is all the same to you, one each side.'

Poor Lieutenant Gruber. I hadn't seen him look so ill at ease since he heard that one of his pals from his window-dressing days had been hit in the Bulge.

'Despite my experience in the touching-up of old masters, I had not formerly realised how coarse was the canvas used by Van Gogh.'

'He probably painted it on the skirt of some old native,' I said.

'Let us hope he washed it first,' the Lieutenant replied.

Denise bade me farewell as I set off on my mission, but not before she had delivered a word of warning to the prisoners.

'If the ransom is paid you will be released more or less unharmed,' she snarled. 'If not – bang, bang, bang.'

They wouldn't let me take baby Mimi with me. They said it was better that the poor child be looked after by women.

'But surely she will get in the way when you are killing Germans and blowing things up?' I said.

Denise would have none of it. 'The worry of being an orphan has already made her look old beyond her years.'

1 JUNE

General von Klinkerhoffen doesn't want to pay the ransom.

My first thought was: If he does not care, why should I? Let there be banging. My second thought was: If there is a lot of banging, there might also be a lot of Big Boobies with holes in them, and Cracked Vases that are more or less impossible to stick back together.

2 JUNE

Michelle cannot stop the bombers. The battery on the radio is flat. We shall have to find the ransom money from somewhere else – or I'll never be able to provide for my o age.*

3 JUNE

I've thought of somewhere else.

Edith has been despatched to borrow all the money in Monsieur Alfonse's Swiss bank account.

4 JUNE

First the bad news. Monsieur Alfonse did not die from the shock.

Now the even worse news. Suddenly he cannot remember the number of his account and the Swiss bank is closed anyway because it is a bank holiday.

How else can we raise the money? Not even Roger Leclerc could forge one million francs by tomorrow. Not

---

* *Unkind critics – and it has to be said that the great man had more than his fair share of knockers – might interpret this piece of exploded text as 'old age'. As if René would think of protecting his own interests at a time like this. The intended word is clearly 'orphanage'. My mother told me he never rested in his pursuit of the interests of the younger generation. It is extraordinary that he never had children of his own.*

good ones, anyway.*

Michelle has a plan that she will outline to me tomorrow for my approval. I am proud of that girl. She has learnt much from the master.

The maître heartily recommends the Boeuf René aux Flageolets to a grateful customer.

There seems to be some confusion here. The billion lire note as shown is of course genuine.

5 JUNE

'I am not going to rob a bank,' I said when she had finished. 'I could get life – or even longer. And then where would everyone be?'

They were too upset by the question to answer immediately.

'In that case we will not get back the paintings and we will be poor forever,' Edith said at length.

'René,' Yvette winked, 'think of the uses you will have for this money ...'

12 JUNE

There we were then, outside the bank. The church clock had just struck twelve. Michelle was keeping watch. Should anyone approach she would hoot like an owl. Personally I think that as leader it was I that should have been doing the hooting, and she the breaking in. But there is a time to lead and a time to stand back, and anyway it was a bit windy so I decided it would be warmer inside.

13 JUNE

Let me explain where I have been for the last few days. I have been locked inside a bank vault.

Leclerc got the door open all right, and we entered the vault. Unfortunately the wind then blew it shut again.

'I still have the plastic explosive,' the old fool said after we'd been there a week. 'We will blow open the door.'

I greeted his words with a mixture of relief and regret. I would be glad to be relieved, but at the same time I was pleased to be able to help Yvette, who suffered from claustrophobia and needed to be held tight while she took deep breaths.

Michelle was waiting outside with Crabtree while all this was going on.

'They have been a long time,' Michelle said at last.

'Do you think we should have a poke?' Crabtree asked.

'A poke?'

'To see what is happening.'

It was kind of them to think of rescuing us but unfortunate that they arrived exactly ten seconds after Leclerc had lit the fuse.

14 JUNE

My troops have recovered from the shock of the explosion, thanks largely to the bottle of my finest cognac they drank when we got back to the café. Personally, I felt better the moment I had counted the stolen money. I've never counted to a million before, even on a good night.

19 JUNE

A tuning-point in my life. I have decided I cannot continue to allow my wife to sing. I am losing customers. She will be heartbroken, but that's show business.

I have a plan. I fetched down my old gramophone from the attic, a box of needles – medium-loud – and a pile of records. Now all I have to do is break the news to Edith.

20 JUNE

No rush. Tomorrow will do.

21 JUNE

Or the next day.

22 JUNE

'Edith,' I said pleasantly, 'I am very worried about
Monsieur Leclerc's piano-playing when he accompanies
you. He does not do your voice justice.'

'I have thought this myself,' she replied.

'It occurred to me that if you were backed by an
orchestra – preferably a big symphony orchestra, a loud
one, conducted by Toscanini ... then your full potential
could be realised.'

I handed Edith a record.

'Toscanini – how wonderful. What is this name – it
looks like Jeanette MacDonald.'

I had to explain that it was just possible that the
MacDonald woman was singing on it a little bit, but the
customers would never notice.

'Your voices are so similar,' Yvette said.

'Of course,' Edith said. 'I model myself on her.'

Yvette started the record. I tapped the bar-top with a
spoon and started to conduct.

Edith sang: 'Love is where you find it ...'

I tapped the bar-top with the spoon.

'Edith – much quieter. You are drowning sixty-four
members of the New York Philharmonic.'

After several false starts I finally managed to get her
to sing so pianissimo that she was scarcely audible.

'Turn your back, Yvette,' I said. 'Tell me who is
singing.'

'I cannot tell. I think it is Madame Edith.'

'Perfect,' I said to Edith. 'You open next month.'

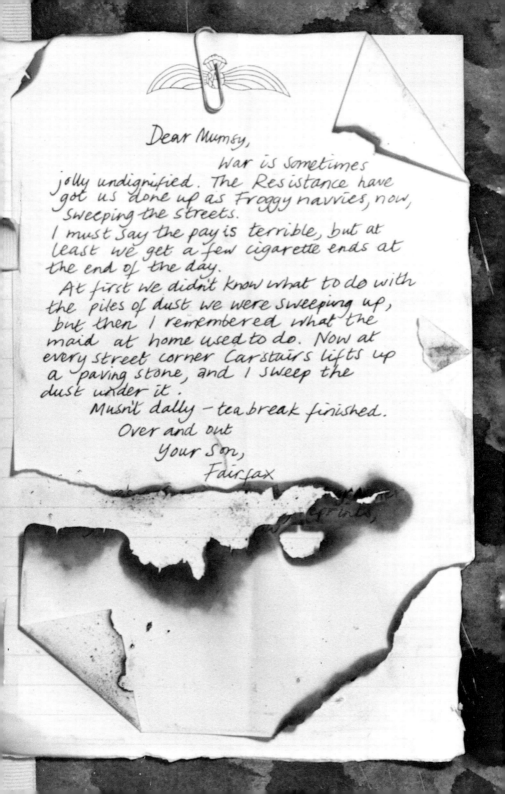

Dear Mumsy,

            War is sometimes jolly undignified. The Resistance have got us done up as Froggy navvies, now, sweeping the streets.

I must say the pay is terrible, but at least we get a few cigarette ends at the end of the day.

   At first we didn't know what to do with the piles of dust we were sweeping up, but then I remembered what the maid at home used to do. Now at every street corner Carstairs lifts up a paving stone, and I sweep the dust under it.

   Musn't dally – tea break finished.

     Over and out

       Your Son,

         Fairfax

Helga is not certain whether it's a gun Herr Flick has under his sinister leather coat, or if he's just pleased to see her.

Edith Artois takes a break from her act to read her next request: 'Four more slices of Emmental'.

26 JUNE

Helga tells me that Herr Flick was looking off-colour this morning. His skin had turned from its usual shade of putty to a more deathly white.

'I have just been to the bank where every Friday I collect my divi,' he told her. 'The strong room has been blown open. One million francs from my personal Gestapo slush fund have vanished without a trace.'

Oh heck, one million francs from his personal Gestapo slush fund. I started to look a little off-colour myself. Helga continued her story.

'But who would have the temerity to do such a wicked thing?' she had asked him.

'Someone who hates me.'

'Everybody hates you.'

'In the Gestapo that is a measure of one's success.'

Nevertheless, he thinks that General von

Klinkerhoffen hates him most, and suspects him of stealing the money.

'I feel very small and alone,' he told Helga. 'You will lend me fifty-seven francs for a ham sandwich and a cup of coffee.'

1 JULY

Crabtree dropped a bumshell this afternoon.

'When you ribbed the bonk there was a wetness,' he said. 'I have drawn poctures of the sispocts. Nobody has soon the poctures because I have not ponned them on the beard outside the Polooce Stootion, but some of them lurk vaguely familiar.'

This is bad nose indeed.

6 JULY

If Flick finds out that we have his money he will have us shot – slowly and painfully. But what can we do with it?

Michelle says the Resistance will look after it. I'm sure they will. We'd never see it again.

Monsieur Alfonse is prepared to conceal it in a tomb, but I am sure he means a vault in a bank in Switzerland.

The argument was settled when Colonel Von Strohm appeared in the square, heading towards the café. He looked cross. Michelle grabbed a couple of notes and vanished like a phantom into the hairdresser. I was left with the rest, and the Colonel was getting closer.

'Hide it down my bosom,' Yvette offered.

'There is no room,' I said.

'We will hide it down your trousers,' Edith said. 'There is plenty there.'

The Colonel and Lieutenant Gruber entered the café just as the last few notes were stuffed into place.

Lieutenant Gruber is bent on opening up a second front . . .

. . . and René reluctantly tries his hand at a little insider dealing.

'Colonel, Lieutenant, what a coincidence,' I said. 'We were just on our way to rescue you.'

'René,' said the Lieutenant, 'I hear a strange rustling sound.

'Mice,' I said.

'I have the strange illusion that it is coming from your trousers.'

'Would you put a mousetrap down *your* trousers Lieutenant?' I asked.

I hobbled off into the back room, unaware that the Colonel had ordered Gruber to follow me. I pulled down my trousers to release all the money, and stooped to pick it up.

'René,' I heard a voice behind me. 'Could it be that I have hit the jackpot?'

I straightened up fast, and made the Lieutenant promise that he wouldn't tell anyone what he had seen. He replied that long underwear was nothing to be ashamed of.

'I am talking about the money,' I said. 'Last night we blew up the bank and stole one million francs to pay a ransom for your release.'

Not for the first time, Gruber was touched.

'You did this for me!' he exclaimed. 'Clearly the money is not safe in your trousers. We must put it down mine. I must make room for it.'

He reached deep into his trousers until his hand hit something firm.

'I think I have found the Van Clomp,' he smiled. 'Please René, take one end of it.'

Cautiously, I held out my hand. I had no idea how big his Van Clomp was going to be. As I closed my fingers around it, I realised to my relief that it was the size of a rolled-up painting.

'I have to be very careful with the Van Gogh,' Gruber added.

'It is very valuable,' I agreed.

'It has very rough canvas.'

As I pushed it down inside my long johns I saw what he meant. We began to transfer the money to his trousers. They were exquisitely tailored, if a little tight. Apparently a dear friend from his old window-dressing days had had a hand in them.

10 JULY

This is getting complicated. I have given the money we stole from the bank to Lieutenant Gruber. He is our deadly enemy most of the time – or in my case, my deadly friend. He is taking care of the money so it cannot be traced to us. In return he has given to me what he believes to be the original paintings, except that they're not, to keep down my trousers. I will give them to Edith to put with the other forgeries.

When the Lieutenant asks for them I hope she does not give him the real ones by mistake. They, of course, are the ones in Mimi's trousers.

You have to be on the ball in this game.

14 JULY

Denise knocked on the window tonight. The Germans are looking for her everywhere. Naturally she had come to the house of the man she loves.

'But what if they find you here?' I asked.

'Then we will die in a hail of bullets, fighting together, in each other's arms.'

'Surely there is somewhere safer?' I protested. 'The bus shelter, for instance – nobody goes there – the service is discontinued.'

Café René

19 JULY

It seems I no longer run a café; I am the proprietor of a refuge for girls on the run. This is not as much fun as it sounds: they are girls of the Communist Resistance.

Miss Denise Laroque, whose description is no doubt being circulated throughout the length and breadth of the country, is hiding in the room of Mimi Labonq, who hates Communists but has accepted my explanation that the fugitive has Militant Conservative tendencies.

Louise, her deputy, is also hidden in my café, despite my protests that I am a bit full at the moment.

'Could you not come back next week?' I asked, quite reasonably.

'There are Germans everywhere. If I have to die, let it be in your arms.'

Of course. How else would a girl want to die? Apparently from the moment she set eyes on me she wanted to run her fingers through my hair.

'Hide me in your bedroom,' she persisted.*

'Unfortunately,' I had to tell her, 'I am sharing that with an elderly member of the staff.'

* *René Artois guarded his privacy intensely, but he was obviously no stranger to the Reds under the bed long before the Cold War had even begun.*

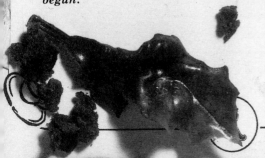

24 JULY

Tonight, for Edith, it was the big one.

'Ladies and gentlemen,' I announced, 'accompanied by sixty-four members of the New York Symphony Orchestra, conducted by Arturo Toscanini, Café Reńe is proud to present ... Madame Edith.'

My wife took centre stage. Monsieur Leclerc, hidden from the audience's view, wound up the gramophone. Unfortunately the old fool also knocked over the pile of records and lost his glasses. At last he signalled that all was well.

I tapped the bar with a spoon. 'Maestro – when you are ready.'

Leclerc sat at the piano, miming sixteen bars of a big piano concerto intro. Edith came in exactly on cue. The voice of Paul Robeson began to sing 'Ole Man River'.

'There is no doubt about it,' said Lieutenant Gruber, 'she is improving.'

Edith Artois does battle with the enemy ...

... and formally accepts Captain Bertorelli's unconditional surrender.

The sun is shining, the scent of summer is in the air. I should not have a care in the world. If I were not hiding two British airmen and two girls of the Communist Resistance and if I had not robbed a bank and stolen one million francs of Gestapo money and if Lieutenant Gruber did not think that I had something for him down my trousers, I probably wouldn't.

Michelle has microfilm of the German invasion plan. The RAF has sent a carrier bird that will fly it direct to London. I expected a carrier pigeon. Silly me. The RAF has of course provided us with a new long-distance duck. And she has given birth to a whole squadron of long-distance ducklings.

The effect on Yvette is not good. 'Oh look at those little babies,' she said. 'What does that make you think of?'

'Orange sauce and stuffing,' I said.

I shouldn't have mentioned the stuffing.

Yvette wants to run away to Paris with the money we stole from the bank. When I told her that the money was now down Lieutenant Gruber's trousers she burst into tears. I had to console her more or less immediately.

Edith arrived with a bowl of potato peelings.

'René! What are you doing with your arms around that girl?'

Stupid woman! Could she not see that Yvette was faint with hunger? That the young, innocent serving girl cried to see good food being given away to the ducks?

'Poor child,' Edith said. 'You must build your strength up. Here, have some potato peelings.'

Poems from the Front
of Hubert Gruber

I must go down to the café again,
To the lovely René in the square;
And all I ask is a little tank
And a joystick to drive me there.

I wandered lonely as a kraut
That floats in tanks o'er bumps and holes;
When all at once I saw a chap,
Mine host of golden wine and Bols;
Behind the bar in the back passage,
Would he like to give me a

Dear Uncle Heinrich,

Thank you for your letter of the 16th

With respect the Gestapo money that was stolen from the bank was not genuine. Yes of course it is the principle of the thing, but do not worry. I will detect the miscreants and bring them to justice – but not as you suggest. Uncle, you cannot expect me to shoot everybody in the town. I am unpopular enough already.

Your loving Nephew

Otto

P.S. By the way is there any chance of a postal order to tide me over

27 JULY

Himmler is very cross with Herr Flick about the missing Gestapo money. Helga thinks it must have been money from the Gestapo Christmas Club Fund. A lot of people will be going without their turkey and sinister trimmings this year if it isn't found.

She says Herr Flick is as mad as a snake because his his uncle is in a moody. He must get the money back quickly before there is an investigation and anybody starts asking questions about the paintings that were supposed to have been sent to Hitler. His plan is to disguise himself and Von Smallhausen as market traders, and try to catch a person spending one of the forged notes. The person will be arrested and interrogated until he leads them to the source. Seeing as I am the source, I am not altogether sure that this is a good plan.

28 JULY

Lieutenant Gruber wants to give the money anonymously to Herr Flick and put an end to the matter. The Colonel would rather not be hasty. After all, a million francs buys a lot of strudel.

29 JULY

Michelle appeared at the window tonight flicking a large chamois leather. My pulse quickened, but not for long. In her other hand was a bucket. It is her new cover. She has disguised herself as a window cleaner so that she can go from house to house without arousing suspicion. I think it will work better when she remembers to put some water in the bucket.

Anyway, she told me only once that she had the microfilm of the German invasion plans in a package. I am to attach it to the leg of the long-distance duck. The duck will transport it to London.

She produced the package. It was as big as a brick.

'For this you will need a long-distance albatross,' I protested.

Luckily the microfilm was only a tiny part of the package. Unluckily, there is a problem with the duck. She and her four little ducks are inseparable. If she is taken away from them she will not reach Calais before she gets post-natal depression.

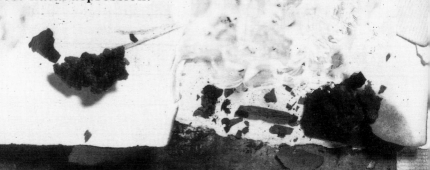

NOUVION RESISTANCE

FROM UNDER THE DESK OF: *Michelle*

CERTAIN RESISTANCE MEMBERS HAVE HAD DIFFICULTY IDENTIFYING THEIR DESIGNATED TARGETS. THE FOLLOWING SILHOUETTES SHOULD HELP DIFFERENTIATE BETWEEN FRIEND AND FOE:

CARRIER PIGEON ONE OF OURS

LONG-DISTANCE DUCK, ONE OF OURS

CAPTAIN BERTORELLI ONE OF THEIRS

LIEUTENANT GRUBER'S LITTLE TANK — ONE OF THEM

READ THIS VERY CAREFULLY. I WROTE IT ONLY ONCE

There are, alas, few mementoes of Michelle of the Resistance. She wrote to the greatest hero in all France during the war years, but evidently only once. I expected something a trifle more intimate than this Resistance circular, but I reproduce it here anyway

1 AUGUST

Denise Laroque is hiding in a wardrobe in the passage outside the bedroom of my wife's mother. I have to be very careful or she grabs me as I go past. This morning I was not careful and she grabbed me by the ball s.*

'I knew you would come to me, passion of my life. Just the sight of your brave face has made me giddy.'

'It is probably the smell of the mothballs that I have just crushed under my feet.'

Denise tells me she wants to kill the woman I am living with, bury her in the garden and hide with me in the sewers of Paris, popping up from time to time to kill the hated enemy. I can hardly wait.

* *Ballisters.*

*Louise of the Communist
Resistance delivers
a secret massage.*

2 AUGUST

Louise is hiding in the next wardrobe along. This morning
she grabbed my buns. I was very upset – they were my
favourite crusty ones, and Yvette had buttered them
specially. Louise told me she had been cooped up all night
thinking of me.

'I am eating these buns so that I might build up my
strength so that we may run away together,' she
announced.

I do not think that two sardines and a bit of cress will
get her very far, but who am I to argue with a staunch
Communist with her finger on the trigger?

She wants to kill Denise, hide her body in a disused
refrigerator and fly away to the Alps where we can drop
rocks on the Germans.

'Unfortunately,' I told her, 'we use our disused
refrigerator, but the moment it breaks down I will let you
know.'

7 AUGUST

Monsieur Alfonse has been to the hairdresser's to have his moustache restyled. The pomade that they use is their own preparation made from badger-grease and rose-petal water. He also had his hair shampooed with an extract of hedgehog to give it body. This has its drawbacks. At the sound of a car hooter it clenches itself into a ball.

M · A L F O N S E

U N D E R T A K E R S

'Twenty-four hour service'

Dear Mutti,

Herr Flick is a genius. We disguised ourselves as fish-sellers today in the hope of catching a French peasant spending forged money. Herr Flick dressed as a fisherman. For me, he provided the costume of a fishwife.

'This looks like a good pitch,' he said to me in the town square. Then he started to call, 'I have the winkles, I have the winkles alive alive-o.' I did so want my disguise to be successful, so I joined him. 'I have the crabs,' I called. 'I have the crabs, alive alive-o.'

'Von Smallhausen,' Herr Flick explained, 'you will drive people away. You are not a good fish-seller.' His words crushed me. 'I am sorry, Herr Flick. Just tell me what to do....'

'Conger,' he commanded me 'conger.'

'Ere we go, 'ere we go, 'ere we go,' I sang, 'ere we go, ere we go, 'ere we go.....'

He hit me with an eel. I just know life would be better if I were taller, Mutti.

Yours under the weather
Bobby Cedric Von Smallhausen

* Historians of the Nouvion campaign will be intrigued to know that Englebert was not in fact the name with which Von Smallhausen was christened. Mutti had much to answer for.

8 AUGUST

Monsieur Alfonse and his restyled moustache have been arrested by Herr Flick and Von Smallhausen. He passed a forged note at the winkle stall and was caught. He protested that he was innocent but, as Herr Flick said, if that was the case then why was his hair standing on end in fright when they shone a desk-light at him?

Michelle is to blame. She used one of the stolen notes at the hairdresser's and the ageing embalmer ended up with it in his change. All I can say is, he must have given the hairdresser an awfully big one in the first place.*

Michelle put up a weak defence. 'For weeks I have not had my hair done,' she said. 'As head of the Resistance I have a position to maintain.'

I'm surprised at her. I expect those who serve under me to be made of firmer stuff.

But she did have a plan. On the radio under the bed of my wife's mother she ordered from London two pairs of 15-denier stockings for herself and a packet of suicide pills for me. The quick ones.

* *Large denomination note.*

9 AUGUST

I don't think it was the mention of suicide pills that made me faint. I have been exerting myself more than usual in the kitchen recently, examining the melons and kneading the dumplings, and I think the effort has taken its toll. All the same, I'd like to know what Michelle has in mind.

10 AUGUST

The duck was ready for l unching.*

'Do you have the long-distance dick?' a policeman asked me as I carried the box into the square. 'I will mauv these peasants out of the wee and make a clear pith.'

'This will go down in history as the turning-point in the struggle of the oppressed people of the world against the jackboots of the fascist imperialists,' Edith said.

It was indeed an impressive moment. Tension mounted as she pulled open the trap. At last, the long-distance duck was free and she waddled out. Four little chicks were close behind. We chased the lot of them around the square but nothing got airborne. Eventually Mummy duck seemed to remember her training, and was last seen walking past the Post Office in the general direction of the coast. I hope she is careful. One German convoy and her family will be orphans.

---

* *René has dwelt upon the melons and dumplings at some length, but I don't think he's planning to get his teeth into any other delicacies. The missing letter must be 'a'. The duck is ready for take-off.*

14 AUGUST

The Communist girls have thrown Mimi out of her bedroom and forced her to sleep in the broom cupboard. I told her to look on the bright side – it is next to the hot-water tank so she'll be nice and warm.

'Blood of my life,' Denise Laroque said to me later in the privacy of her wardrobe, 'my heart pounds like a sea of passion crashing on the rocks of my desire. I have but to look at you and I see clouds scudding across the moon, trees bending on a tropical shore ...'

Mon Dieu, I cannot even swim.

15 AUGUST

'My passion is greater than her passion,' Louise tells me. 'Inside me surges a tidal wave of need that is waiting to crash upon the firm rocks of your manhood and to tumble us both into a whirlpool of ecstasy.'

I must remember to leave a rubber ring by my bed.

She wants me to dangle out of my window at midnight. She will dangle out of hers, and we'll meet on the parapet and make wild, abandoned love. It will certainly give the neighbours something to talk about.

She has gone now to do five hundred press-ups so that she will be able to go the distance. What is it about me that turns nice girls into hooligans? Can nobody resist?

CAFÉ RENÉ

16 AUGUST

I wish Lieutenant Gruber could.

He and the Colonel are worried that the missing money will be traced back to me. Well actually, they're worried that it will be traced back to me and then back to them. The Colonel has short-listed a choice of two plans.

The first is for Edith to make a pasty into which I will put a suicide pill. We will chuck it through the bars of Monsieur Alfonse's cell. He will gobble it up and that will be the end of it.

The other is for me to take the pill myself. But, as I said to Lieutenant Gruber, I am sure the undertaker will be happy to die for France.
And if I know Edith's pasties, we shouldn't need to waste a suicide pill.

Monsieur Alfonse cannot stand the torture.

Monsieur Alfonse has had a heart attack at Gestapo headquarters. Helga was alone with him when it happened, explaining to him that she wanted to help him escape because she also was in possession of some of the money and didn't want Herr Flick to find out. Monsieur Alfonse wanted proof that this was not just a Gestapo subterfuge. Helga opened her jacket and shirt to reveal a black lacy bra stuffed with big ones.*

But that wasn't the end of it. She also lifted her skirt to reveal a hacksaw blade, which happened to be concealed in the top of her black silk stocking, which happened to be attached to frilly black suspenders. The old boy's dicky ticker flicked at a quick lick, and he is now in the German wing of Nouvion General Hospital.

Well-wishers congratulate René Artois on his achievement of First Prize in the 1942 Nouvion Knockwurst Festival.

---

* *At least ten thousand francs' worth, by my estimation.*

19 AUGUST

Crabtree was wicking down the street when suddenly he licked at his watch and saw the tomb. Good groocious, he sod to himself, I should be spooking to my opposite nimber in London on the roodio. It was a quitter-past six.

He came into the café and I took him upstairs to the room of my wife's mother. His truncheon was swinging from his belt as we entered and the sight of it seemed to take Fanny back to the old days. She made a grab for it but Crabtree said he had new time to west.

''Allo, 'allo – secret agent Crabtree cooling,' he said. 'Connect me to Wombledon one-sox, one-sox.'

'Receiving you lewd and clore,' said the voice at the other end. 'Hold the loon, I will connoct you.'

My God. There was another one at the other end.

We eventually got through, but it was MacFisheries, and they were shut.

'Bigger,' said Crabtree. 'A wrong nimber. I will go and chock it in my address bike.'

It was at this moment that I spotted the mouth of my wife's mother wrapped around the pasty in which was the suicide pill. I at once drew Edith's attention to a few chores that needed doing at the other end of the room, but then she, too, saw the pasty and the game was up. The old bat had taken a bite but it came out intact. She hadn't had her teeth in.

20 AUGUST

Read this very carefully – I shall write it only once. Michelle of the Resistance has got a plan that involves fitting the bravest man in all France with a false bottom.

It is clear that we must get into the hospital to rescue Monsieur Alfonse before he talks. To do this she suggests that we disguise ourselves as ambulance workers, pushing a trolley with a concealed compartment. In it will be a dummy of Monsieur Alfonse wearing pyjamas. On top of the trolley will be a patient requiring emergency treatment. The idea is to exchange Monsieur Alfonse for the dummy. The emergency case will then demand a second opinion in another hospital and he will be pushed out.

I have volunteered to be the emergency case who lies on top of the rescued undertaker. I would do the same for anyone. With the possible exception of Lieutenant Gruber.

TEMPERATURE CHART

140

21 AUGUST

120 What a pity Michelle did not co-ordinate her plan with Helga, who at that very moment was inventing an exploding bedpan with which to eliminate Monsieur Alfonse. It was to be activated by remote control.

100 'How do we know when the bedpan is in position?' Lieutenant Gruber asked her.

'In it there is a microphone,' Helga barked. 'We can 80 hear the voice of the nurse when she gives it to him.'

60

40

20

0

DAY 1   DAY 2   DAY 3   DAY 4   DAY 5   DAY 6   DAY 7   DAY 8

N O U V I O N

G E N E R A L   H O S P I T A L

NAME: M. ALFONSE

TEMPERATURE CHART

140

120

100

22 AUGUST

We have arrived at the hospital. I was on the trolley and the dummy was under it. Another dummy was pushing it – Crabtree, dressed in a long surgeon's coat and mask, large, loose rubber gloves and a pair of rubber boots.

'It is a good disgeese,' he said. 'I can wick anywhere in the hospital without areesing sispoocion. All they can see is my eebrews.'

The bravest man in all France on his way to another secret operation.

DAY 8

O A I PITAL

NAME: M. ALFONSE

26 AUGUST

I still have not got over the shock. Not so much the trauma
of the explosion, more the terrible sight of Lieutenant
Gruber and the Colonel dressed as nurses. One of my
fondest fantasies has been shattered.

The two Florence Nightingales appeared on the ward
just as we were bundling Monsieur Alfonse under the
trolley. Helga and Captain Bertorelli were outside, up
against the hospital wall. Helga was bending over the radio
set. Bertorelli was priming his plunger. Both were ready
for a big bang.

'Bedpan to Control,' Gruber whispered into the
container, 'Bedpan to Control.'

'Hello Bedpan,' Helga replied, 'we are ready to
activate.'

Michelle, Edith and Crabtree disappeared off to retrieve
the dummy from Monsieur Alfonse's room, leaving me
alone on the trolley in a corridor. It wasn't long before a
German soldier appeared. I whispered a hasty warning to
Monsieur Alfonse, and in the panic his equipment began
to bleep wildly. To allay suspicion I disguised the noise by
whistling a tune. I chose the 'Ritual Fire Dance'. The
soldier looked at me with a strange expression on his face,
then finally walked on.

I breathed a sigh of relief, but the danger was not past.
The idiot Crabtree had parked the trolley right outside the
operating theatre. A German surgeon poked his head
through the swing doors. He wore gloves and a gown, and
a pair of the thickest pebble glasses I had ever seen.

'Where is the French peasant woman?' he asked,
feeling his way along the wall. 'I am ready to perform the
Caesarean.'

I will be in Lieutenant Gruber's eternal debt for finding
Monsieur Alfonse's bed at that precise moment,
positioning the badpan under it, and sending the signal for
Bertorelli to press the plunger.

27 AUGUST

The explosion was the biggest I had heard since the night
Edith found me demonstrating to Yvette how to escape
from a German position. The surgeon scarpered for
shelter, and Monsieur Alfonse began to push me like the
clappers.

It is a quarter past one in the morning and I have just
crept into my café wearing a hospital gown after trudging
five miles from the Nouvion General Hospital where I was
in the maternity ward.

Am I really writing this? Maybe it is all a terrible
dream.

No, it is not. The draught blowing up the back of my
gown tells me it is true.

28 AUGUST

I had just put away my diary in the early hours of yesterday
morning when Lieutenant Gruber appeared at the café
door.

'Are you open?' he asked
'Partly,' I said, adjusting the gown.
The Lieutenant beamed.
'It is for the air-raids,' I said. 'One has to be ready to
leap in and out of one's clothes very quickly. But why are
you here at this hour, Lieutenant? Shouldn't you be in your
little tank, practising a few manoeuvres with Clarence?'

Gruber told me that Monsieur Alfonse had been
eliminated. So now we are all in the clear.

'Do you fancy a little something to celebrate?' he
offered.

I turned to go to the bar but suddenly thought better

of it. 'Er, not in the circumstances. I have to put the cat out.'

The Lieutenant was very persistent. He said he could put it out with me. He too has a little cat.

'Really? What is it?' I asked.

'A ginger tom.'

29 AUGUST

Yvette is full of apologies for driving off in the ambulance without me. Apparently they put Monsieur Alfonse in the back and thought I was with him.

'Did nobody stop to pick you up?' she asked.

'Yes,' I said. 'Three times. In the end I had to hide in the woods.'

Yvette had just begun to show her sympathy when Edith appeared with a burning candle in her hand.

'René! What are you doing with that girl?'

'Stupid woman, can you not see that she has been overcome by the anaesthetic on my operating gown?'

Edith apologised and told me to help Yvette upstairs. She would follow with the candle.

'Not while I'm wearing this gown,' I said. 'You help her upstairs and I will follow with the candle.'

30 AUGUST

Helga told me that Herr Flick suspects that the stolen money is hidden in Monsieur Alfonse's mortuary. He has despatched Von Smallhausen to gain entry and conduct a search. To do this without arousing suspicion, the miniature interrogator will be disguised as a corpse. I must warn Yvette to watch out for a little stiff.

31 AUGUST

Suddenly everyone wants to get rid of the money. And nobody wants to carry it.

Gruber thinks Helga should take it in her knickers.

'We cannot have Helga going through the town dropping notes of large denominations from her underwear,' said the Colonel. 'People would wonder what sort of army we are running.'

Gruber had another idea. 'If I may say so, Colonel – nobody would suspect that a man with feathers in his hat would have anything of great value down his trousers.'

'How-a you like a smack in the face, uh?' said the Italian.

The Colonel and Lieutenant Gruber convinced Bertorelli that he should bring the money to me in his trousers. This was a great pity. I didn't want it. It was hot money. And it would be even hotter after an hour or two in an Italian's southern region.

1 SEPTEMBER

There is a dark side to the Colonel that I never suspected.

He has ordered Helga to keep the Italian under close observation. The moment he departs for the café she is to inform him. The Colonel is going to snitch to the Gestapo, who will have him arrested. In one stroke the money will be returned and the Colonel will be rid of the irritating wop.

2 SEPTEMBER

Crabtree has a message for me. It seems that Michelle is in the town square with a new escoop apparootis for the British earmin.

'When I give her the secret sognal she will appear like a phantom out of the newt,' he said.

Some secret. He went to the door and gave a long, loud blast on his whistle.

'Listen very carefully,' Michelle said as she slipped up the back passage. 'I shall say this only once. The Germans are about to put into action a new and terrible secret weapon.'

I was tempted to say that if it was as secret as Crabtree's signal it would be all over Europe by Tuesday.

'It is a very big bum,' said Crabtree.

Apparently it is a new type of landmine, a development of the Mark Five. The Mark Sox, according to Crabtree. The Resistance has captured two of them and hollowed them out. As the police interpreter explained, Michelle's plin is to ploce the two British earmin inside. The bums will be loaded on a bummer on a dick night, and they will be dripped over Ongland.

It occurred to me that this might well kill them, but apparently that has been thought of. The earmin will wear parashats.

'The lods of the bums will be secured by stell nits. Each earmin will have a spinner. As they descond they will unscrew their nits,' Crabtree continued.

Well, it will be one way of pissing the time.

'Then they will remauve the lod and immediately jump and open their parashats,' he concluded.

Frankly I want no part in this crazy plan. I am resigning from the Resistance.*

* *One of René's little jokes.*

Dear Mumsy,

           I say old thing,
I've been thinking about this new escape
plan. I'm a bit windy about it. For
instance, how do we find our nuts in
the dark? Carstairs and I have
been looking into this frightfully
carefully in the last few days.
    We've decided to cover them with
     luminous paint
       Yours in a tizz,

          Fairfax

My mother is surprised to see that her memories of René don't hold a candle to Mimi's.

5 SEPTEMBER

Mimi wants to know when these girls of the Communist Resistance are going to leave us. She wants her room back so that we can fly away together on a magic gossamer cloud of happiness and enchantment. I have a shrewd suspicion she is talking about her duvet.

Oh Mimi – so much passion bottled up in such a small container.

6 SEPTEMBER

Great news for all those girls wanting to fly away with their bosses on a magic gossamer cloud of happiness and enchantment: the girls of the Communist Resistance have held a branch meeting and by a democratic vote of twelve to three they are moving to Abbeville.

'If I should die your name will be found carved on my heart,' Denise told me.

That's nice, as long as she doesn't put my address on as well.

As for Louise, she said that as soon as it is safe she will kill Denise and come back and take what is hers.

'What have you left behind?' I asked helpfully.

'You. I make you a solemn promise that you will be kidnapped, bound hand and foot, and brought to me within a month.'

'I'm a little tied up as it is,' I replied.

7 SEPTEMBER

The Colonel was very eager to snitch on Captain Bertorelli this morning but Herr Flick wasn't answering his phone. Typical secret police; never there when you need them.

All the Colonel could get was his answering machine. 'This is a recorded Gestapo message,' said the voice. 'I am not taking calls at the moment but you may leave a message on the revolving wax disc. Please speak after the gunshot.'

Pretending to be an anonymous French peasant, the Colonel left the tip-off that the stolen money was in the trousers of a man with feathers in his hat who could be found at Café René.

'I would tell you more,' the Colonel said, 'but my money is running out. Pip, pip, pip, pip.'

I'm tired. Must remember to give Yvette a note about the shopping.

The old pillow-stuffer looks like having his feathers ruffled.

8 SEPTEMBER

Woke up to find that Yvette had given me one.

Dear, romantic child. She does not realise the candlesticks are only electro-plated. She will be heartbroken. It was certainly a shock to me when I took them to the pawnbroker's.

I had just finished reading when the Itie Bertorelli arrived at the café. He went straight over to Edith.

'I have-a for you a lot of something which once-a René had but no longer he got,' he whispered.

Feathers?

He said he want-a to take her upstairs, take-a his trousers down and-a give her one million francs.

I wasn't convinced that this was a fair rate of exchange, so to save him the stairs, I took the money myself. Mimi hid it in the oven.

Moments later Lieutenant Gruber arrived and told me the Gestapo would be arriving any minute to arrest the man with the feathers in his hat who had the stolen money in his trousers.

A minute later Leclerc arrived, disguised as an old pillow-stuffer. He was indistinguishable from the genuine article, as usual. In the pillows were parachutes for the airmen. In his hat were the feathers.

Herr Flick was seconds behind him. He was wearing his sinister black overcoat and an expression that said, 'I am as mad as a snake.' He had received information that

the man with feathers in his hat had down his trousers
something of interest to the Gestapo.

'It is I, Leclerc,' the old fool pleaded with me.

'I have never seen you before in my life,' I said.*

11 SEPTEMBER

It is many years since I sat down alone, rolled up my
sleeves, and let my hands glide up and down the old
instrument. So many years, in fact, that at first I thought
perhaps I wouldn't remember how. But the moment my
fingers started their rhythmic caress, it all came back to
me.

Attracted by the sound of my efforts, Edith crept into
the room and slipped her arm around me.

'You had a strong left hand in the old days,' she said
with a glint in her eye, 'and the fingers of your right hand
seemed to be everywhere.'

It is true. There was not a note that was safe. I played
in all the bars those days. I was known as Syncopated
Sydney. For all I know, in some bars, I still am.

* *It may have been after this incident that René drew up the notice I
reproduce here. It was placed behind the bar at the Café René:*

NOT WANTED!

AT ANY PRICE!

THIS MAN IS A MASTER OF DISGUISE AND SHOULD BE AVOIDED WHENEVER POSSIBLE. ON **NO** ACCOUNT SERVE HIM ALCOHOLIC LIQUOR!

THE OLD PILLOW-STUFFER

THE OLD KNOCKWURST PURVEYOR

THE OLD CHEESE-SELLER

THE OLD FORGER

THE OLD PUTTY-SELLER

THE OLD MOUNTAINEER

THE OLD AMISH ACCORDIAN-PLAYER

THE OLD PIANO-PLAYER

THE SILLY OLD FOOL

THE OLD COBBLER

R

The reason that I was once again tickling the ivories was sad but simple. Monsieur Leclerc has been arrested by the Gestapo because Berlin suspects he has something of great value down his trousers. I can only think that this rumour was started by my wife's mother.

'Do you remember how I sang to you under the old willow tree by the river?' Edith asked.

How could I forget? As I played and she began to sing, it all came flooding back.

'Yes,' I sighed. 'The trouble I had lugging the piano down there.'

The emotion of the occasion was too much for Edith.

'Oh René,' she purred, 'let us get married again! What have we got to lose?'

'Nothing we have not lost already,' I said.

'Are you afraid that I might be unfaithful to you and run off with a younger man? René, I am in the autumn of my life. There is the hammer-toe on my right foot, the bunion on my left, the first murmurings of sciatica in my right hip . . .'

'You might still hobble off with a younger man.'

Edith promised that from now on she will be by my side twenty-four hours a day. I thought immediately of one or two times and places when that might be a little inconvenient, but I didn't have the heart to tell her.*

'Edith, I do not know a man who could resist such an offer, but you forget Denise Laroque. She is wild about me. She would shoot any woman whose lips even brushed against mine.'

'Oh René, you are my wonder man. Always you think only of me. Just let me kiss those magic fingers.'

I told her it was not safe. One of Denise's friends might have seen us through the window. I made her pull my hand down behind the piano and do her nibbling there.

---

* René is so considerate of his wife's feelings. It was man's work in the cupboard under the stairs. And it goes without saying that he wouldn't have wanted his dear wife to be present while he was lifting tenderloins in the larder or humping in the coal cellar.

12 SEPTEMBER

There was a terrible smell wafting around the café this morning. It was too early for Lieutenant Gruber to have been in wearing that special aftershave of his – lily-of-the-valley with a hint of diesel oil – and, as far as I knew, my wife's mother was up in her room.

No, she wasn't. She had decided to cook herself a big baked potato, the one I had concealed behind the cistern in the bathroom – the one that contained the spy camera for photographing the German invasion plans.

She was baking it in the oven.

Thanks to the stupid old interfering bat, the best part of the hidden one million francs had gone up in smoke.

It wasn't so much the money that I cared about. I knew it was forged. But I wasn't going to take the blame for the camera.

'I shall tell the Resistance that it was your fault, you deaf old crone,' I said.

'Then I will tell the Germans about the paintings, the airmen, the stolen landmines,' she snarled. 'I can finger you buddy and get you sent to the big house just like that . . .'

She snapped her fingers to emphasise the point.

I decided to give her the poison pasty treatment again on the first day she remembers to put her teeth in.

13 SEPTEMBER

Good moaning. Guess who had bad nose for me this morning?

A poster has been pisted on the wills of the Town Squeer. It is a picture of Roger Leclerc without his trousers. It reads: 'Unless the money stolen from the Gestapo is returned within twenty-four hours this man will be shot in the Town Square.'

There are worse places to be shot, as I know to my cost. Leclerc may find this small consolation of course, but what can we do?

We cannot give back the money; it is so hot it's cremated. We cannot forge some more; the forger is the one they are going to shoot. Time is of the essence. Every minute counts. We must act at once.

14 SEPTEMBER

There again, if he is not here to play the piano, then Edith will not be able to sing.

15 SEPTEMBER

But on the other hand, under threat of death he may reveal our connections with the Resistance and we could all be shot in the Town Square.

I know Leclerc. He is a brave man. He will hold out until the very last minute, bravely hoping that the money will be returned.

And when it is not? He will drop us in it.

CAFÉ RENÉ

16 SEPTEMBER

Lieutenant Gruber enquired after my health tonight. I looked pale, he said, and my hands were trembling.

'It is the worry of the war, you know,' I said to him. 'Hoping that you are going to win.'

Gruber told me he had come to help me to give the money back to the Gestapo so that the pianist could be set free.

I told him about my wife's mother, the baked potato and the money that was now in ashes.

'This is not good news, René. But I could very likely help you if you could just let something else drop.'

Lieutenant Gruber has a gift for seeing things from a different and often surprising angle. I put it down to his artistic leanings.

'On the other hand,' I said, 'he was not a very good pianist.'

I could see that the Lieutenant had more on his mind than the fate of geriatric piano-players. At length he came out with it.

'René, do you have any information that may lead to the return of the missing landmines? If they were returned I am sure I could arrange the release of the pianist. Remember, René, my door is always open.'

I didn't doubt it.

17 SEPTEMBER

My wife's mother is determined to rescue her lover, Roger Leclerc. She stole a handgrenade from the Germans and was setting off to storm Gestapo headquarters in her bathchair when Edith intercepted her.

'I will pull out the pin with my teeth,' the old bat spat, 'and stick it through their letter-box.'

Unfortunately she'd left her teeth by the bedside and Edith managed to talk her out of it.

It's a great pity, she would have died a glorious death.

Fanny finally locates her spare set of teeth.

18 SEPTEMBER

For Monsieur Leclerc, I fear, the war will very soon be over.

Herr Flick has orders from Berlin requiring the Colonel to provide a firing squad to execute the wandering pillow-stuffer. The order was signed by Heinrich Himmler in person.

'I keep-a this,' said Captain Bertorelli when he was shown the piece of paper. 'Me, I collect-a the autographs.'

It seems that because Lieutenant Gruber ran the last firing squad, it's the Italian's turn this time. Bertorelli's men will pull their triggers at seven o'clock tomorrow, and Leclerc will have played his very Last Waltz.

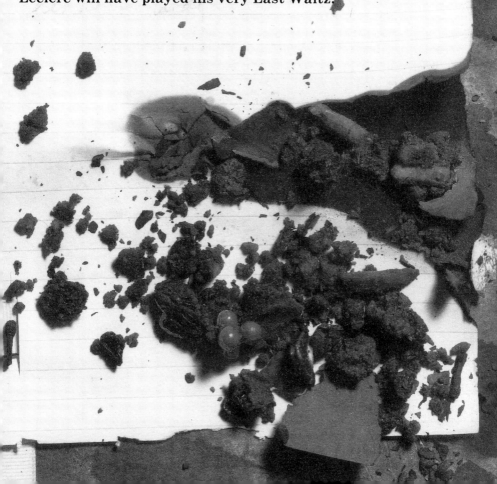

19 SEPTEMBER

It was ten minutes to seven and there was no sign of Leclerc.

Michelle had instructed the RAF to drop the money to us last night. Crabtree wetted all night in the woods flushing his titch. The bummers pissed overhead but the clods were very loo and it was a bit figgy.

Then it was five to seven and there was every sign of Monsieur Leclerc. He had been marched into the square and put against the wall.

'If the money is not returned in two minutes the wandering pillow-stuffer will die,' hissed Herr Flick. His words echoed off the stone walls and shopfronts of downtown Nouvion.

One minute to seven. I felt so sorry for the old boy. Even if the Italians missed, Michelle had guns trained on him by her markswomen in case he cracked at the last minute and dropped us in it. If the RAF were late, she didn't want to take any chances.

The church bell began to toll. At the seventh stroke, with the tension so electric that even the feathers on Captain Bertorelli's hat stood on end, the air was shattered by a long, loud droning noise that grew and grew in intensity.

Had Leclerc's nerve finally cracked? No. My eyes were drawn to something fluttering in the breeze. Banknotes. Thousands of them. The RAF had arrived at last, and money rained down from a squadron of bombers. One million French francs – minus, of course, the small commission deducted by the Nouvion Chamber of Commerce for services rendered.

As one uniformed bystander so rightly remarked: 'Just in the nick of tomb.'

20 SEPTEMBER

'What do you fancy this time?' I asked Yvette in the cellar tonight. 'Smooth and velvety, or for a change maybe, a bit of the rough stuff?'

'Oh René,' she said, her fingers tight around one of my tumblers as I reached for the jugs. 'You make it so hard for me. I will love whatever pleases you, so long as it makes my heart sing and my knees tremble.'

Tasting the local vintages so that I may choose a house wine for my café is indeed a difficult task. Some wines tonight were too good for the peasants. Others were simply too bad for them, though good enough for the Germans.

At last I got my hands on something firm and full-bodied.

'Put another pint of anti-freeze in each barrel,' I told Yvette. 'And then you can come and help me with the laying down.'

Crabtree in the dark.

Not altogether to my surprise, I awoke this morning with an enormous smile on my face.

A great load has been lifted from my shoulders. The Gestapo have received back their money, Leclerc is free and they are no longer searching for Monsieur Alfonse. All I need now is for my wife's mother to spontaneously combust and I'll have the grand slam. But for the moment we are free to make as much money out of the war as we can.

'René!' Yvette called. 'Michelle wants you in the back room.'

Oh heck. I knew it could not last.

Michelle was always proud of her big berets.

22 SEPTEMBER

Michelle was wearing dirty dungarees and a false moustache, and was carrying a brick menacingly in each hand. The very sight of them made my eyes water.

It is her new disguise. She is a builder.

'If the Germans find me here,' she said, 'I am repairing your window.'

'But it is not broken,' I said.

Very carefully and only once, Michelle chucked one of the bricks through a pane.

'It is now,' she said.

She brought bad news. 'When we stole from the Germans the landmines in which the British airmen are going to escape we had to remove one thousand kilos of high explosive. You are probably wondering what happened to the explosive.'

'To tell you the truth,' I said, 'I never gave it a thought.'

She went on regardless. The explosive was hidden in a pudding factory, she said, and the Resistance had secret information that this factory was to be commandeered by the Germans for the manufacture of frozen strudel which was to be sent in food parcels to the Russian Front. Naturally the Resistance could not leave this explosive to fall into German hands. And – surprise, surprise – they have therefore arranged for it to be delivered to my café.

All one thousand kilos will be disguised as a product of the factory. To wit, five hundred Christmas puddings.

Are these people out of their minds?

I told Michelle I wanted nothing to do with her puddings, and that was final.*

---

* *This is not like René. Usually he would have been the first to volunteer his help with Michelle's puddings. Perhaps he had a headache.*

23 SEPTEMBER

Michelle went away sulking. Soon afterwards she sent through my window a coded hate letter. It was wrapped around her unused brick.

'What is the matter with you?' I finally deciphered. 'All you have to do is sit in your comfortable café and hide a few paltry Christmas puddings. How would you like to be a twenty-four-hour emergency plumber with putty under your finger nails, burning your hands on the blow lamp, drinking tea from a paint kettle and sitting down on a pile of bricks to eat a doorstep sandwich with a twelve-inch spanner in your back pocket?'

I'm sorry to say I softened at this point. But I wasn't half as sorry as Yvette.*

24 SEPTEMBER

Would you believe that I have received a bill for repairs to a broken window?

25 SEPTEMBER

Two broken windows?

---

* *I had not previously realised the depth of my mother's feelings for Michelle.*

26 SEPTEMBER

Lieutenant Gruber was rather in his cups today.

'I think the Colonel and I were not cut out for the military life,' he confided sadly. 'Every night the Colonel prays that Hitler will not invade England. That damned English weather will be fatal for his rheumatism. And the food! Before the war I was one month in a small hotel in Croydon. Do you know, René, they eat faggots for breakfast?'

I imagine he left Croydon in rather a hurry.

27 SEPTEMBER

The Lieutenant is a mine of information in his present mood. General Von Klinkerhoffen told him that it has come to the ears of Hitler that two of the new Mark Six landmines are missing from this district. Hitler has of course flown into one of his familiar rages.

'Has he eaten the carpet?' Gruber asked the General.

'He has done a lot of no good to a reproduction of the Bayeux tapestry.'

'Do you think he has a screw loose?'

'It is my opinion that a whole Meccano set has fallen apart in there.'

Dear Mutti,

Herr Flick is so beastly to

Yesterday he was on the telephone. 'Yes mein Führer,' he was saying, ' no, mein Führer, of course, mein Führer. I understand, mein Führer. I am very grateful to you, mein Führer. Goodbye, mein Führer.'

'Was that the Führer?' I asked him.

'No it was my mother.' She was checking to see if my underwear which she has knitted for me is a snug fit.'

'And is it?'

'Mind your business.'

This is typical of how he snaps at me. It's so unfair. I try my best.' What more can a man of five foot two do?'

Your loving overgrown fruitbat

Bobby Cedric Von Smallhausen

P.S: Thank you for the stacked heels. Unfortunately Herr Flick noticed that I was six inches taller and ridiculed me without mercy. I now use them as bookends for my collection of Trenchcoat Monthly.

Monsieur Alfonse offers Fanny a special deal.

29 SEPTEMBER

Monsieur Alfonse has delivered to my café fifty-eight exploding Christmas puddings concealed in a coffin.

My wife's mother took one look at it and went screaming back upstairs as fast as she could hobble.

'It's an ill wind,' she shrieked to nobody in particular.

'We'd better open the windows,' I said.

Dear Mutti,
    Berlin expects the Gestapo to find the missing landmines. We are just the boys for the job, I tell Herr Flick. It is his opinion that much of the subversive activity in Nouvion is conducted at René's café.

    'Gestapo spies tell me that there are frequent comings and goings in the larder,' he said to me.

    'I do not remember mentioning this,' I said.

    'You are not the only sneaky pebble on the beach,' he snapped.

    He produced a map. 'We must find the position from which we can observe these things. I have decided upon the church tower. From there we can see directly into the larder and the upstairs windows.'

    You know how much I have always wanted to look down on the Resistance. I realised now was my big chance.

    'Herr Flick, you are a marvel,' I said. 'You will go a long way with your brain.'

    'And you will go nowhere with yours,' he said.

Your Son,
    Bobby Cedric Von Smallhausen

30 SEPTEMBER

Helga tells me that Herr Flick and Von Smallhausen have removed their clothes in order to follow the Führer's instructions. They have disguised themselves so that they can merge into an ecclesiastical background.

Herr Flick is dressed as a monk, complete with open-toed sandals that he made himself. Von Smallhausen is similarly dressed, but with a halo hanging over his head. It was part of the set.

Herr Flick has ordered Helga to bring to the church tower, at four o'clock, coffee and sandwiches to sustain them during their vigil.

'What will you be doing in the church tower?' she asked.

'Snooping.'

Helga finds the lengths to which Herr Flick will go to achieve his ends very exciting. She wanted to kiss him, but unfortunately the rules of the order to which he belongs forbid any physical contact with girls.

Crabtree arrived this afternoon with two expleeding Christmas poddings.

'I suppose they are down your trousers as usual?' I asked wearily.

'Do not be redoculous,' he said, throwing aside his cape to reveal a lovely pair of puddings slung around his neck. 'Do not drip them or they may go off bong.'

'How do I account for the very obvious presence of sixty Christmas puddings in the larder in September?' I asked Yvette as we were struggling to get our legs over them.

'Say we are members of a pudding club,' she suggested.

The girl from the hat shop with the big berets announces that she is in the club.

2 OCTOBER

Edith said there was a girl outside who wanted to see me. She told my wife it was a private matter.

'I am glad you are open,' she said as she came in. She was wearing a raincoat, under which she appeared to be wearing a very large bump. She pointed at it. 'I did not want to leave this on your doorstep.'

'I deny ever having seen this girl before,' I said.

'I am not the only one,' she said. 'Six more girls are outside.'

I hesitated.

'We are in the club,' she said.

This was going to take some explaining.

The six girls came in, all with big bumps.

'And there is a busload coming at seven o'clock,' said one of them.

I was calculating my chances of making it to the door without being scythed in half by Edith's kitchen knife when one of the girls threw open her coat.

'One exploding pudding,' she said proudly.

Phew! I felt like all my Christmases had come at once.

René casts an anxious eye over my mother's explosive puddings.

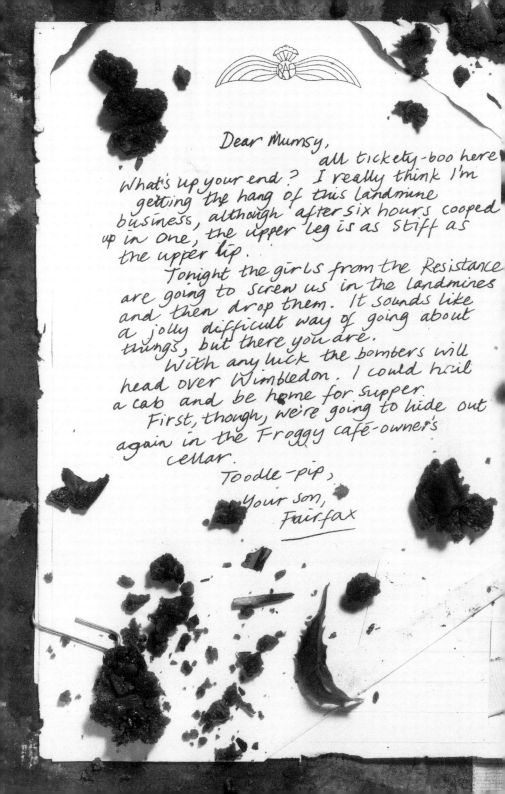

Dear Mumsy,
                              all tickety-boo here.
What's up your end? I really think I'm
   getting the hang of this landmine
business, although after six hours cooped
up in one, the upper leg is as stiff as
the upper lip.
      Tonight the girls from the Resistance
are going to screw us in the landmines
and then drop them. It sounds like
a jolly difficult way of going about
things, but there you are.
      With any luck the bombers will
head over Wimbledon. I could hail
a cab and be home for supper.
      First, though, we're going to hide out
again in the Froggy café-owner's
      cellar.
              Toodle-pip,
              Your son,
              Fairfax

3 OCTOBER

Brother Otto has had a mishap in the church tower. A rising rope caught him unawares and now he is suspended by the clappers.

Brother Englebert is not much better off. One of the church bells has fallen and completely enveloped him.

Dear Mutti

Sorry if the writing is wobbly but its very dark in here. A bell fell on my head an hour ago.

I know it was an hour ago because I just heard Herr Flick say so. A tiny gap has opened up between the bell and the floorboards of the church tower. I think perhaps Herr Flick is starting to winch up the bell to save me. Maybe he values me after all.

'I would have expected some whimpering noise by now,' I heard him say to Helga.

Whimper, Mutti? Me? The long distance limping champion of Westphalia three years running?

'There is not much room for air to be admitted through the small crack,' I heard Helga reply. 'Perhaps he has suffocated.'

'I see his hand protruding,' said Herr Flick. 'Tread on it.'

Helga did so.

'Aaagh!' I responded.

They started to ask me questions. I was to bong once for yes, and twice for no.

'Do you wish to have a ham sandwich?' Helga shouted.

I bonged once.

'With mustard?'

I bonged twice.

'Hold the mustard.'

Through the crack came one end of a thick ham sandwich. Then it got stuck.

'Herr Flick,' Helga boomed, 'the sandwich is too thick.'
'Then remove the ham.'
She did so.
   I took the plain bread and sucked on it gratefully.
Half an hour later, in a supreme feat of strength,
Herr Flick lifted the bell clear. But instead of the
rapturous reunion I had had in mind, my superior
announced that he had bad news for me.
   'You have been squashed well below the minimum
height required for members of the Gestapo,'
he said. 'Let me have your resignation in the
morning.'

   I'm very upset now, so I'll write again
shortly.
                Bobby Cedric Von Smallhausen

10 OCTOBER

It is midnight, and a terrible disaster had occurred. The British airmen are still concealed in empty beer barrels in my cellar instead of being airborne somewhere over England, waiting to be dropped from a German bomber. Herr Flick and his assistant Von Smallhausen are in the Heinkel instead.

It seems that while he was suspended by the clappers in the church tower Herr Flick saw something suspicious in the builder's yard next to the café. According to Helga he and Von Smallhausen went to investigate, found the landmines, and decided to occupy them.

It was Herr Flick's opinion that under cover of darkness the Resistance would transport the mines to their secret headquarters. As soon as they heard somebody speaking in the French language, they would leap out, subdue them, arrest them and march them to Gestapo headquarters. Frankly I think they are as mad as hatters but that is the Gestapo for you.

But I disgress. The Colonel also located the mines, thanks to Lieutenant Gruber maintaining his position at my café.

He got Bertorelli's men to load them on to a truck and take them to the Luftwaffe base, not realising that they were stuffed full of men in sinister leather coats.

Michelle discovered that the mines had been moved.

'Do not worry,' she said, 'I have a plan.'

I started to worry.

'We have an agent at the base. We know precisely the position of the landmines. They are in the landmine stores. The barrels with the British airmen inside them will be taken to the air force base. They will be allowed in as a consignment of beer for the Sergeants' mess which is being sent with your compliments. Once past the guard, it will be a simple matter to get them into the landmine store because it is next to the Sergeants' mess.'

'I have to hand it to you, Michelle,' I said. 'You've come up with some ridiculous plans in your time, but you and your girls are very, very brave to do this.' 'Women are not allowed in at the base. You are going with Leclerc.'

We loaded the barrels containing the two British idiots on to barrows and set off for the base. The third British idiot led the way.

'Halt!' shouted the guard at the gate. 'What is the password?'

'On these two trilleys we have two borrels of boor for the Sergeants' miss,' said Crabtree as fluently as ever. 'They are a goft from Roné's Cifé. If you rood this handwroten nute all will be explonded.'

'What is he talking about?' the guard asked me.

'He is from the mountains,' I explained. 'This is a present of beer for the Sergeants' mess.'

'Pass, friend,' was the immediate reply.

Leclerc, Crabtree and I stole into the landmine store. I wanted us to find out quickly which were the empty landmines, get the airmen into them, and clear out of there like bats out of hell.

'I have a hammer,' said Leclerc. 'I will hit the casings and we will find out which ones are hollow.'

I stopped him just in time. There is definitely something wrong with that dithering old fool. The lights might be on, but there's nobody home.

Crabtree located the landmines – the empty ones with crosses on them. We were just about to pull off the lids when we heard the sound of boots on concrete. We hid. Two Germans arrived in service overalls, pushing barrows. Into each barrow they put one of the landmines.

'Dimnation,' whispered Crabtree. 'Footed at the eleventh ear.'

With heavy hearts, and heavier wheelbarrows, we headed for home.

My mother attempts to satisfy the appetites of the British airmen.

11 OCTOBER

I am not normally a drinking man, especially at half past eight in the morning, but my nerves are shot to pieces. I feel like a cat that has used eight of his nine lives. Why am I in this state? Firstly, I have a cellar full of 258 exploding Christmas puddings. Secondly, the British airmen, who were supposed to leave last night, are back following yet another British Intelligence cock-up.

Between you and me if there was enough money in the till I would leg it over the border with Yvette and start fighting my war in a different theatre. Since she is twenty years younger than me it might be an operating theatre but it's a risk I've had to come to terms with.

I still have the painting of the Fallen Madonna with the Big Boobies by Van Clomp together with the painting of the Cracked Vase with the Big Daisies by Van Gogh with which to finance our undercover activities, but could I leave my possessions? My café? My friends? My wife?

We heroes of the Resistance sometimes have to make these sacrifices.

12 OCTOBER

Michelle informs me that London has come up with a bold and daring plan to get the British airmen back to England.

'I see,' I said. 'What hare-brained scheme are they suggesting this time? Are they sending a submarine up the canal at midnight?'

'It was supposed to be a secret.'

I do not believe it.

13 OCTOBER

I still do not believe it.

14 OCTOBER

Perhaps I should not have underestimated the brilliance of the British Navy. The brave sailors are bringing a midget two-man submarine.

I can't help wondering: how do you fit four men into a two-man submarine?

Dear Mumsy,

I say it's all go.

Carstairs and I have just been measured for diving helmets. The jolly matelots are coming to get us; we're coming home astride a midget sub. Come and wave us in at Dover if it's a nice day, won't you?

The plan is for the Froggy café-owner to take us to the canal disguised as eel-fishers. He is a member of the Nouvion Fishing Club and apparently you fish for eels at night. Under cover of darkness he will row us and the diving helmets to the RV where we will meet the good old RN.

Goodness knows what'll happen if the Germans find us with two diving helmets. Perhaps the Froggy will say that the eels aren't biting and that we are going down to make sure that the bait is still on the hooks.

Anyway, must dash — it's all around the Resistance that Carstairs and I are pretty damned good divers, and for some reason the girls suddenly seem dashed eager to get us down into the cellar....

Shiver me timbers!

Your son, Fairfax.

17 OCTOBER

I was with Yvette in the back room when I told her I could no longer take the strain.

She was open mouthed.

'We will take the paintings,' I said. 'We will head for Switzerland and hide out in the mountains until the war is over. Nobody must suspect a thing. From now on we will not even talk to each other. When I am ready I will leave you a note telling you the time of the train.'

Silently, we had one last embrace.*

* *My mother confirms René's earlier claim that heroes of the Resistance would often do this, particularly at times of great tension. All these years later I still find it strangely touching.*

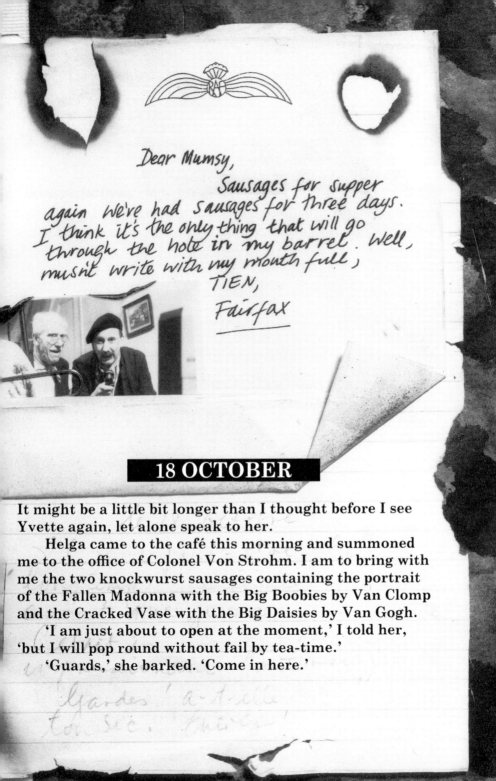

Dear Mumsy,
           Sausages for supper
again we've had sausages for three days.
I think it's the only thing that will go
through the hole in my barrel. Well,
musn't write with my mouth full,
                    TIEN,
           Fairfax

18 OCTOBER

It might be a little bit longer than I thought before I see
Yvette again, let alone speak to her.

Helga came to the café this morning and summoned
me to the office of Colonel Von Strohm. I am to bring with
me the two knockwurst sausages containing the portrait
of the Fallen Madonna with the Big Boobies by Van Clomp
and the Cracked Vase with the Big Daisies by Van Gogh.

'I am just about to open at the moment,' I told her,
'but I will pop round without fail by tea-time.'

'Guards,' she barked. 'Come in here.'

12 NOVEMBER

Let me try to explain why it is several weeks since I last made an entry and why I am now sitting in the toilet of the 11.15 express to Geneva with a pile of paper in my hand.

It is a long story, the paper is French Railways economy size and in short supply, and another passenger is banging urgently on the door. So I will be as brief as I can.

It turned out that the Colonel wanted the paintings back because the General wanted to send them to Berlin because Hitler wanted to give Eva Braun one. I offered him the forgeries, but it seemed the Führer was taking no chances: he was sending an art expert to authenticate the paintings. But there was worse to come. The General had demanded that the Colonel shoot the peasant who had been hiding them.

'Do not worry, René,' the Colonel said. 'We have known you for a very long time. We all feel very close to you. We have decided to allow you to escape.'

'Oh thank you, Colonel,' I said. A couple of days to tie up a few loose ends at the café and say goodbye to old friends, and I'd comfortably catch the Weekend Saver to Zurich.

RAILWAY PROPERTY

'We will give you sixty seconds start, commencing now. Go.'

I went.

Unbeknown to any of us at the time, however, Herr Flick had been informed by his godfather Heinrich Himmler that Hitler could not have telephoned General Von Klinkerhoffen because for the last week he had been shacked up in a tent deep in the Black Forest having the secret nookie with Eva Braun. I always thought Hitler was above that sort of thing, but it seems he is crumpet-mad.

Herr Flick told Helga and Von Smallhausen that he planned for them to recover the paintings while in transit by train to Berlin.

'We will sell them and then we will run away to a tropical island,' he said. 'There we will lead a simple life together dressed in banana leaves as we frolic in the surf under the warm sun. Does this appeal to you?'*

* As things turned out, there was a last-minute change of plan. Suddenly in late 1945 they decided to honeymoon on the upper reaches of the Amazon Basin, and I'm told that they were so taken by the natives that they decided to make their home there.

Herr Flick ordered Helga to sell their canvases of The Fallen Madonna with the Big Boobies and The Cracked Vase with the Big Daisies and they opened a small cinema, The Flick House, on the proceeds. If they had had possession of the originals it would have been a large cinema.

I hear that to this day they play re-runs of old Erich von Stroheim movies to packed audiences. Helga shines her torch into the customers' eyes and instructs them to buy ices and soft drinks, whilst Herr Flick spends much time in the projection room, operating the machinery. Von Smallhausen appears during the intervals, playing a small organ. Sometimes, carried away by the applause, he overstays his welcome and gets beaten over the head with a large knockwurst by the front-of-house manager.

'All except the sea,' said Von Smallhausen. 'I am not a very good swimmer.'

The Swedish art expert, Yup Von Hoop De Hoop, did indeed verify the authenticity of the two paintings.

'My client will be most satisfied,' he said to General Von Klinkerhoffen as he handed the German one million marks in the form of twenty gold bars.

'I will take the paintings personally to Geneva,' said Von Hoop De Hoop. 'The night express has in its guard's van a safe. My destination and mission is known only to you and to my client. I don't think that we have anything to worry about.'

Experience has taught me never to think . . .†

---

† *It is not clear at this point whether René had run out of paper or if he realised that the other passenger's need was greater than his own.*

13 NOVEMBER

Little did Von Hoop De Hoop know that Helga was behind the curtains and had heard everything.

Me, I was on my way to the police station. So, minutes later, was General Von Klinkerhoffen. In fact I had only just arrived when I had to dive under the counter to escape discovery.

'Heil Hitler,' he said to the policeman on duty at the desk.

'Hole Hotler,' came the reply.

The General said he wanted to store some not very important papers in the police safe. His own safe at the château had been blown up by the Resistance. He sent the policeman from the room while he opened his briefcase to effect the transfer. I watched astonished as he pulled out twenty bars of gold.

'If you tell anyone about this you will be shot,' he told the policeman when Crabtree returned to the room.

'My lips are soiled,' was the reply.

The General left and Crabtree was called away with his lidder to roscue a Siamese pissy up a tree. I opened the safe with a spare key I found and helped myself to four gold bars.*

Back at the café, I scribbled a hasty note to Yvette.

'I have nicked a fortune in gold. We must leave tonight for the mountains. Be on the 11.15 Geneva Express. Here is the ticket for the sleeper. Your own René.'

I put it in a buff envelope and gave it to Leclerc to give secretly to Yvette.

Then I wrote Edith a tender note to say goodbye.

'Goodbye,' the note said.

---

*   *René again worries about how to finance his war effort.*

*Madame X prepares
herself for action.*

14 NOVEMBER

Then I added: 'It is best for both of us that I leave you. Do
not grieve for me. Monsieur Alfonse will make you a fine
husband. Yours faithfully, René Artois.'

I put it in a white envelope and gave it to Leclerc. I
said I hoped he wouldn't mix them up.

'Don't worry,' he said. 'This envelope is buff – for your
bit of stuff.'*

He has such a way with words.

I wish he had had more of a way with envelopes.

'This is the buff – for the old bit of rough,' he reminded
himself as he gave Edith the wrong one.

'This one is white – for the bit of all right,' he said as
he gave Yvette the other one.

* *I have questioned my mother closely about this reference, which seems
to me to hold the key to so much of what went on undercover. 'René,'
she has always responded, 'the war was very complicated, and there
are some things that we simply cannot bring out into the open, even
now.'*

To make matters worse, Edith then left Yvette's note by the till and Mimi found it. She, in turn, thought I had written to her.

'Aah,' she gasped in that small but perfectly formed way of hers. 'I would follow that man to the ends of the earth.'

Colonel Von Strohm and Lieutenant Gruber felt the same. They boarded the Geneva Express dressed as guards. Helga boarded it dressed as a beautiful spy.

'I have reserved one first-class sleeper to Geneva, please,' she said to the ticket-seller.

'Name?' he asked.

'Madame X.'

The Colonel's plan was for Madame X to insinuate herself into the compartment of the art expert, Yup Von Hoop De Hoop, drug his wine, and get the keys to the safe in the guard's van. Lieutenant Gruber would then substitute the forgeries for the original paintings.

The plan might have worked, had Herr Flick and Von Smallhausen not also been aboard the train.

'Members of the public are not allowed in here,' a steward told them as they barged into the buffet car.

'We are members of the Gestapo,' said Herr Flick. 'Take off your white monkey jackets and leave the train.'

'But it is moving,' the steward protested.

'Then you had better start running before you touch the ground.'

15 NOVEMBER

It is way past midnight. I have woken in a cold sweat. There are some things that a man sees and does in wartime that are not easily forgotten. I will try and tell you about them tomorrow.

16 NOVEMBER

No I won't.

17 NOVEMBER

Oh, very well.
  I, meanwhile, was just arriving in my compartment.
Our bunk, 4B, the upper one, was curtained off.
  The curtain moved a little as I undressed.
  'Is that you?' I whispered.
  'Yes, my love,' came the reply.
  There was a wonderful smell of perfume.

'I have poured a whole bottle over myself,' said the woman of my dreams. 'I feel like a girl.'

'You are a girl,' I cooed.

'Can you get up without a ladder?' she asked me.

As if she didn't know. I took off the rest of my clothes. Well, I said to myself, this is the first night of the rest of my life. I pulled aside the curtain.

The look of joy on Edith's face still haunts me.

'René, I cannot believe this is happening,' she said.

Neither could I.

The train was travelling at seventy miles an hour so I decided I could not throw myself off. It was a decision I came to regret.

18 NOVEMBER

I discovered afterwards that Mimi, Yvette and Leclerc had also somehow managed to join the party. The moral is: one should never put anything in writing.*

I got rid of Mimi by saying that the best thing for her was a quick jump. After a lot of explaining, she finally understood that I meant from the train into the river alongside.

Leclerc told me only once that Michelle was going to drop two exploding Christmas puddings down the funnel of the engine as we went under the bridge at Abbeville. I was just wondering what else could go wrong when the lights went out and there was an earth-shattering bang. It was that kind of evening.

Edith and I made it home across the fields. Luckily she

---

* *Except, presumably, if you take the precaution of concealing the result inside an exploding Christmas pudding.*

didn't find out that our serving girls had also been on the train.

Poor Yvette came all the way on a borrowed pair of roller skates.

Monsieur Leclerc came most of the way with her, except that just outside Nouvion he broke the balls of his bearings.

Mimi, too, made it back – soaked to the skin and covered in greed weed. I put my arms around her shoulders to warm her up.

'Mimi,' I said, 'your bosom is wriggling with delight.'

'It is a trout,' she said, reaching into her bra and pulling out a fish.

25 NOVEMBER

It has crossed my mind that I rather thought I would be in Switzerland when the General discovered that the gold had gone. Now I am in Nouvion. We could all be shot. I must go and put it back.

'Do not wirry,' Crabtree said to me. 'I have squoozed into the lock hard-sitting glue. If he cannot open the soof he will not knee that it is gin.'

I said that I was considering leaving by the next train.

'There are no troons,' he said. 'The one that was derooled by the Christmas pidding is still blicking the loon.'

This is not my day.

26 NOVEMBER

Nor this.

But at least Edith has had a brilliant idea. We have in the cellar exploding Christmas puddings. Her plan is to squash one into the lock, light the fuse and stand well back.

29 NOVEMBER

The Colonel and Lieutenant Gruber have recovered the original paintings of the Fallen Madonna with the Big Boobies by Van Clomp and the Cracked Vase with the Big Daisies by Van Gogh and have secreted them inside a four-foot tall statue in the Colonel's office of a blackamoor with a screwable head.

Helga also reports that the forgeries have been recovered by Herr Flick who put in their place two other forgeries.

Life, it seems, is returning to normal – except that this time I seem to have been cut out of the action.

30 NOVEMBER

General Von Klinkerhoffen paid a visit to the Colonel's office this morning. He wanted Lieutenant Gruber to take his little tank to the police station, pick up the safe which contained some not very important papers, and transfer it to the château where the unimportant papers will be safe.

'Will that be all?' the Colonel asked.

'No, this statue, I rather like it. It would look nice in my château.'

'But General,' the Colonel protested, 'it is such a cheap and ugly thing.'

'Are you questioning my taste? I will take it. Guard – put that statue in my car.'

That'll teach them.

There has been another big bang and again it wasn't exactly the kind I enjoyed.

We went to the police station as planned, with an exploding Christmas pudding.

'I will witch out of the window,' said Crabtree. 'If anyone comes this woo I will give you two wonks.'

Edith pushed half the pudding into the lock and lit the fuse. We ran for cover, not noticing that Crabtree was wonking in the corner. Gruber had arrived. Bertorelli and his men were heading into the police station to help lift the safe into his little tank.

'I think the fuse has gone out,' said Edith. 'It has stopped fizzing.'

Just to be on the safe side, we ran like the clappers out of the back door.

Straight into Lieutenant Gruber.

'Oh, René, I keep meeting you in the most unexpected places,' he said.

'I was just reporting a missing hen,' I said.

The Lieutenant offered me a spin in his little tank on the way back to the Colonel's.

'Well, that is a very kind thought, Lieutenant, but this time I will give it a miss if it is all the same to you.'

Bertorelli stepped forward.

'Me, I have never been-a in-a the German tank. I travel-a with you.'

I could not stand idly by.

'Lieutenant,' I said, 'perhaps the Captain would like to drive the tank while you come and have a drink with me.'

'Oh, an invitation I cannot refuse.'

'You watch-a your Capitano go off in-a cloud of smoke, eh?' Bertorelli called to his men from the turret.

'Don't give it too much throttle,' Gruber cautioned him, 'otherwise you will get a little backfire.'

The tank exploded.

Bertorelli emerged from the wreckage in blackened underwear.

'I give him too much-a throttle,' he said.

2 DECEMBER

All's well that ends well. Captain Bertorelli lost his uniform, the feathers from his hat, and his no-claims bonus, but General Von Klinkerhoffen salvaged his gold from the wreck – and fortunately he did not get his hands on the four bars I stole earlier. With great cunning Yvette and I have melted them down in the kitchen and moulded them into a new weight for the cuckoo clock. Everyone admires its shape and length, particularly Lieutenant Gruber.

For the Lieutenant of course the loss of his little tank was a terrible wrench. He'd had so many happy moments in it. But fortunately the General was so pleased to recover his gold that he has ordered him a new model. Gruber is beside himself. When it arrives from the showroom it will be the only tank in the Corps with a G registration.

3 DECEMBER

Sadly, there are two slightly sour postscripts to the affair. The first is that the General now knows that four of his gold bars are missing. The second is that the finger of suspicion apparently points at me.

The Colonel, fortunately, has decided to do a deal. He will not enquire too closely into the whereabouts of the gold if I agree to help him with a little problem that he has.

'Colonel, it is as good as done.'

'The General has commandeered a statue in which we had secreted the original painting of the Fallen Madonna with the Big Boobies by Van Clomp and the Cracked Vase with the Big Daisies by Van Gogh. The General has taken the statue to his château. You are going to recover the paintings for us.'

'But I am just a humble café-owner,' I backtracked rapidly on my hasty promise. 'I do not get invited to the château. And I am a rotten burglar.'

It went without saying that Helga had a plan. The General is giving a dance which will be attended by the Generals who are planning the invasion of England. He has booked for this occasion the Palm Court Quartet from the Hotel Excelsior in Deauville. They will not arrive. The Colonel's men will stop them at a checkpoint. Their place will be taken by a scratch crew from the Café René.

'But Colonel, we are not musicians.'

'Helga has thought of this.'

In the château there is, apparently, a most up-to-date electric amplifying system. The Colonel has records of the quartet which Helga will play upon a concealed turntable.

Dear Mutti,

Herr Flick is being mean to me about my application for promotion. He yelled for me to go into his quarters this morning. In his hands he held my form.

'You are of course aware that you are only a provisional member of the Gestapo?'

'Yes Herr Flick.'

'You have applied here for promotion to Grade 3 Officer, are you prepared to take the test?'

I have been in training, Mutti. It is my dearest wish to move up the ladder.

Herr Flick sat me down in the chair opposite him

and switched on the spotlight so that it shone in my face.

'The subject that you have chosen is Hitler. You have 30 seconds to answer five questions, starting now.'

'One. What was Herr Hitler's occupation before he became Führer?'

'Painter.'

'Correct. What is regarded as his best work?'

'The iron railings outside 37 Winklestrasser.'

'Correct. What was the name of the barber who created his silly hairstyle?'

'Pass.'

'Correct. Herr Ludwig Pass. You have scored ten points. Stand up. You will now perform the physical tests. Are you ready?'

'Yes, Herr Flick.'

I opened my coat. I was wearing PT shorts and a singlet.

'You have failed,' he said. 'Now pay attention. It is my belief that the purpose of the Officer's Dance at the Château is to further the plot to blow up Hitler.'

'We will infiltrate ourselves into this shindig. We will obtain the names of those present and their photographs. Here is the camera that you will conceal upon your person.'

It was quite a big one, Mutti, I asked him where he suggested I hide it.

'It is up to you, Von Smallhausen,' he said with characteristic superiority and disregard for my feelings. 'If you are unsuccessful you will also fail your "concealing a camera" test.'

Oh Mutti, what can a man do.

urs up to his neck in it,

Bobby Cedric Von Smallhausen

We from the café will only appear to play. We will set up our orchestra near the statue, and while we are only appearing to play we will unscrew the head, take out the paintings and replace the head.

'But how can I do this with everyone looking on?' I asked.

'That, René,' said the Colonel, 'is your problem.'

'Get your friends in the Resistance who you do not know to help you,' quipped Helga.

I think they have entirely the wrong idea about me. All I want to do is run my café and lead a nice quiet life until the war is over.*

12 DECEMBER

Michelle says the Germans have a new machine for encoding messages. It is called Enema.

It is incredible the lengths the Germans will go to in order to pass messages.

13 DECEMBER

Correction, it is Enigma. London want us to nick it from the Parson's Nose. That is secret radio code for the headquarters of the General.

Michelle has a plan. And if I had ten francs for every time I have written that, I would be a wealthier man than even Monsieur Alfonse.

The Enigma machine is in the room next to the salon where we of the Excelsior Quartet will be knocking them dead in the aisles tomorrow night. Mimi is to be concealed in the case of the double bass. I will place it near the door.

---

* *And, of course, do his bit for France. As usual René is selling himself short.*

When the revelry is at its height Mimi will climb out of the case, slip into the room, grab the machine and throw it out of the window where members of the Resistance will be waiting below to catch it in a blanket. She's as bright as a button, that girl. She thinks of everything. She doesn't need me around as leader any more.

'Michelle,' I asked modestly, 'could you not possibly find me a desk job in the Resistance?'

'René, the girls could not survive without your movements underground.'

I have to say that I've had no complaints about my movements above ground either.

Herr Flick inspects Helga's accessories before escorting her to the Gestapo dinner/dance.

14 DECEMBER

Plans, it seems, are all the rage. Edith's is that when we set up our instruments we conceal somebody in the piano and place it near the statue.

'Edith,' I reasoned, 'we are a quartet. You will play the violin, I will play the piano, Monsieur Leclerc will play the cello, Mimi is in the case – who is going to play the bass and who is going to hide in the piano?'

'I could hide in the piano,' said Yvette.

'But who will hold open the lid while you reach out to unscrew the head of the statue?' Mimi asked.

'And that will still leave somebody to play the bass,' I said. 'Edith, your plan will not work because you are still short of two people.'

It was at that moment that there was a knock at the door and in came Monsieur Alfonse, the old undertaker with the dicky ticker and the tricky truss, and the British agent Crabtree, the idiot who thinks he can speak our language.

16 DECEMBER

I wish I could report that all had gone according to plan.

The dance was indeed a glittering occasion. All the top brass were there. So, at the Itie table, were all the top feathers. Herr Flick and Von Smallhausen had successfully infiltrated the gathering dressed as maids, carrying trays of snacks. Von Smallhausen had a very pronounced bosom.

From where I was sitting at the piano, I could see and hear everything.

'Are your sausages prepared?' Herr Flick asked his fellow maid.

'The sticks are firmly thrust into them.'

'Have you tested your camera?'

'Not yet.'

'Then do so.'

I watched in amazement as Von Smallhausen squeezed one of his bosoms. A lace pocket in the other bosom flew open, revealing a lens. It shut again very quickly.

'Good,' said Herr Flick. 'You have ten feet of film nestling in your left booby. Make the most of it.'

They circulated with their sausages and the Excelsior Quartet struck up. Everything went well to start with. Then the idiot Crabtree got carried away and launched into his party piece, a slightly less than perfect impersonation of Maurice Chevalier.

19 DECEMBER

I am very close to a complete nervous breakdown.

For the last few days I have been harbouring once again the original canvases of the Fallen Madonna with the Big Boobies and the Cracked Vase with the Big Daisies – as well as the secret coding apparatus called Enigma. The Resistance had been trying to get it to England by placing it in a wine barrel and floating it into the town drain to be picked up by a two-man midget submarine.

To do this the entire population of Nouvion were supposed to flush their toilets at one and the same time. Needless to say, there was a cock-up. The barrel that they put into the drain contained not a coding machine but some underwear belonging to Yvette which even as I write is probably in the hands of the head of MI5 who is probably trying to decode it.

He will find nothing of interest, except that Yvette is very well built.*

20 DECEMBER

We are no longer trying to send the Enigma machine to the experts in London.

Instead, the experts are going to come here to examine it. They will be dropped by parachute and disguised as policemen. My heart sinks.

When they arrive at the café these agents will make themselves known by means of a secret sign. They will brandish their truncheons in a special way as if they were, well, truncheons being brandished in a special way. Anyway, it is not a gesture that will go unnoticed.

'You will then give us a signal and we will deliver the machine,' Michelle said.

'What will be the nature of this signal?' asked Edith.

'You will place a red cycle lamp in the window of the bedroom of your mother.'

'A red lamp! What will the neighbours think?'

---

* And that, as René implies, is no secret.

'You can say she is being repaired by a road gang,' I suggested.

When the signal has been sent, the Engima machine will be delivered by – who else? – another of their agents disguised as a Spanish accordion-player.

21 DECEMBER

The Enigma machine has now been missing for three days and, from what I can gather, the wires to Berlin have been smoking. Hitler is electrified with fury at General Von Klinkerhoffen. He has delivered an ultimatum. If the machine is not recovered within twenty-four hours the General is to be sent to the Russian Front.

The General has decided that he prefers the Nouvion climate, and has therefore delivered the Colonel an ultimatum of his own. Either the machine is recovered before Christmas Day or I, as the most prominent and likeable figure in the town, am to be marched to the square and shot. I wonder if there is time to commission a quick opinion poll to show that when it comes to prominence and popularity, you can't beat a good piano player like Roger Leclerc?

23 DECEMBER

One of my Christmas wishes came true this afternoon. Edith was arrested by the Gestapo and taken off for interrogation. Unfortunately, so were Yvette and Mimi.

I'll spend the next twenty-four hours or so planning my heroic rescue. There's no way I'll find replacement staff at this short notice.

Helga begins to wonder whether she has arrived at the wrong party.

24 DECEMBER

Lieutenant Gruber arrived early this evening dressed in Helga's uniform. At first I assumed it was his way of getting into the festive mood. But no, he came to warn me that Colonel Von Strohm had reacted badly to the General's ultimatum.

'There have been one or two very serious developments, René,' he said.

'So I see,' I replied.

'The Colonel confiscated my uniform in case I should

tip you the wink. I pinched this while Helga was having a bath.'

The Colonel had taken the view that he must obey orders and start peasant shooting unless the Enigma machine is returned. He's chalked up six of our names for starters; at eight o'clock tomorrow morning his men will arrest a café-owner, his wife, his two waitresses, and the piano-player.

Lieutenant Gruber and that little smile of his that René finds so unsettling.

'Chuck in the undertaker,' the Colonel had ordered Helga.

'Who's going to bury them?' she asked.

'Shoot him last.'

As the Lieutenant spoke I gazed up at the Christmas tree that Yvette and I had so lovingly decorated before she was taken away. I had a sudden vision of myself being hung up by the balls.

'This looks like being a very unhappy Christmas,' I said.

The Lieutenant grabbed a menu and covered his face. Helga had finished her bath. She was now advancing on the bar wearing a greatcoat and tin helmet.

'Helga,' I greeted her, 'what a pretty helmet. Are you on manoeuvres?'

The reply came through clenched lips. 'No. I am on tranquillisers. My uniform has been stolen. Look.'

As she opened her coat I could see immediately that she was right.

'I suspect Lieutenant Gruber took it in order to warn you of your impending fate.'

'I am sure it could not have been Lieutenant Gruber,' I said. 'He would have taken the underwear as well.'

Fortunately, Yvette and Mimi returned to the café just as things were hotting up. Edith was with them. Something rather extraordinary had happened. Herr Flick had administered to them a truth drug in a tea-bag, a new German invention by Baron Von Tetley. I recognised it as having been distilled from the sweat glands of the Patagonian fruit-bat. Unluckily for the Gestapo it had been a faulty batch. The three were released after lying about their age and emitting a series of high-pitched squeaks.

Mimi had been affected the worst. She went instantly to the larder and hung upside down by the hams.

I looked at my watch. It was almost time to don my fancy dress for the Christmas Eve celebrations. I was coming as Toulouse Lautrec. I wondered how long it would take to get to the Swiss border on my knees. Unless the Enigma machine was returned, I had less than twelve hours before the party was over.

At that moment, things really started to go with a swing. The two British agents arrived dressed as policemen, truncheons at the ready. That idiot Crabtree

Herr Flick tells Edith that there are some things he definitely does not want her to reveal.

joined them and there was much excitement. Apparently they had been at longwodge school together.

By the time Monsieur Alfonse and that old fool Leclerc turned up, dressed as Spanish accordion-players, the

truncheons were going full blast. The Enigma machine was concealed in one of the accordions.

'We will arrost the moosicians and take them into the back rim where we will disciver its secrets,' Crabtree told Michelle, who had appeared like a phantom out of the evening.

'You will disciver them only once,' I said. 'The General, the Colonel and the Itie Captain are coming across the square.'

Michelle and the Polooce made a bee-line for the back room with the machine. Captain Bertorelli made a bee-line for Lieutenant Gruber.

'You,' he said manfully, 'how-a you like the good time with the big-a de hero?'

'You must forgive me,' Gruber replied, 'but I am not very keen on moustaches.'

It was the first I had heard of it.

I was heading to the door for a breath of fresh air as General Von Klinkerhoffen decided enough was enough.

He placed a hand on my shoulder and ordered the Colonel to prepare for my immediate execution.

Herr Flick and Von Smallhausen entered with guns. For a moment I wasn't sure whether this party was going to be a total success.

The Crabtree appeared from the parlour dressed as Father Christmas.

'Gentlemen, I have good nose,' he said. And for once he was root. 'The Resoostance, who have no idea of Roné's exoostance, have just throon the Enigma machine through the window of the back rim.'

There was a crash of breaking glass.

'That must be it now,' I said. I thought seriously about giving my guests a drink on the house.

'The matter is now closed,' the General said. 'Now I must call my tailor to cancel my winter uniform.'

'Again I am thwarted,' Herr Flick grimaced.

'So am I,' Von Smallhausen squeaked.

Herr Flick had the last word. 'Your thwart is smaller.'

31 DECEMBER

Needless to say, my Christmas was as active as ever. My stocking was full of little goodies and, despite rationing, so was Yvette's.

Lieutenant Gruber's were too, by all accounts, until Helga insisted that he return them to her in time for Herr Flick's traditional Yuletide interrogation. He holds it in his dungeon immediately after Hitler's Christmas speech.

The Colonel celebrated, as always, with the flying helmet, the egg whisk and some wet mistletoe. From time to time he nipped down to the cellar to make sure that his knockwursts were in safe hands.

That idiot Leclerc only emerged once from the bedroom of my wife's mother. He was disguised very convincingly as the ghost of Christmas Past.

I found the sight of Mimi hanging from my bedstead a little alarming, especially after dark, but I got used to it. After a while she began to remind me of the early days of my marriage to Edith.

The British airmen are also still hanging around, of course. They must be the only two turkeys to have made it past Christmas.